Congo Warriors

Congo Warriors

MIKE HOARE

ROBERT HALE · LONDON

Typeset by Saxon Ltd., Derby
Printed in Great Britain by
St Edmundsbury Press, Bury
St Edmunds, Suffolk and bound
by WBC Bookbinders

Contents

To the memory of
Colonel E. A. S. (Paddy) Brett DSO MC TD, RTR
The Happy Warrior

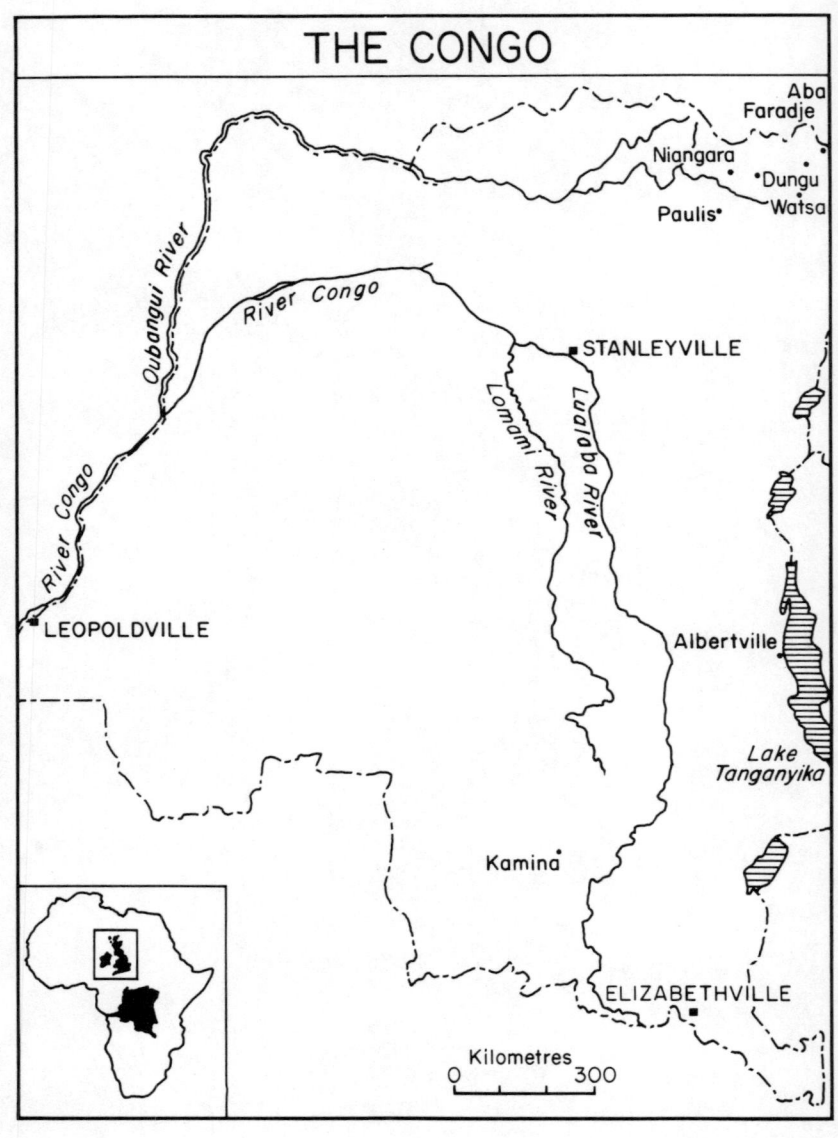

THE CONGO

Aba
Faradje
Niangara
Paulis•   •Dungu
                  •Watsa

Oubangui River

River Congo

STANLEYVILLE

River Congo

Lomami River   Lualaba River

LEOPOLDVILLE

Albertville

Lake
Tanganyika

Kamina•

ELIZABETHVILLE

Kilometres
0   300

Introduction

Prior to 1960 the Belgian Congo was a little-known African country, but in that year momentous events took place which brought it under the world spotlight and changed its destiny for all time. It is this period, from 1960 onwards, which forms the backdrop to the stories which I tell in this book. But first a quick look at the recent history of the Congo, which, as the professors say, need not detain us long.

In 1873 Henry Morton Stanley began his exploration of the Congo, under the aegis and at the personal expense of King Leopold II of the Belgians, with a view to opening up the country to European trade. Six years later the king, seeking to consolidate his claims in the territory, established the International Congo Association. This was at a time when European countries were scrambling for colonial possessions in Africa. The disputes that arose led Prince Bismarck to convene the Berlin Conference of 1885 at which the delimitations of the new African colonies were proposed, debated and finally promulgated. Partly to maintain the balance of power and partly as the result of intense diplomatic lobbying by King Leopold, the International Congo Association was recognized as an independent sovereign state by the USA and thirteen European powers. They granted it sole jurisdiction over the Congo. With the authorization of the Belgian Parliament this vast territory, nearly one million square miles in extent, now became not a Belgian possession but the personal property of the king. It was renamed the Congo Free State.

King Leopold ruled the Congo Free State for the next twenty-three years amid reports of great progress on the one hand and great brutality on the other, but when he died in

1908 the Congo Free State was officially transferred to Belgium as a colony. It became the Belgian Congo and remained a colony until 30 June1960.

The country had been blessed with fabulous mineral wealth, a 'scandal of riches' as one Belgian geologist described it, most of it discovered in the days of the Congo Free State. Copper was found in abundance in Katanga. Industrial diamonds and gem stones in Kasai. Tin, manganese, tungsten, tantalum, coal and iron were all unearthed in Katanga, with gold and ivory in Oriental and elsewhere. Great mining houses were established which developed this amazing wealth so that, for example, in the 1940s the Congo provided seventy-five per cent of the world's cobalt and sixty per cent of its uranium. The uranium used in the production of the first atom bomb in 1945 came from the Shinkolobwe copper mine in Katanga. And apart from its mineral wealth the Congo was immensely rich in timber of all sorts, copal, palm oil, coffee, rubber, cotton, citrus fruits and a variety of smaller crops such as peanuts, sorghum, soya, raffia and kapok. The Congo was a veritable treasure chest. Little wonder then that the western world and the Soviet Union should take more than an academic interest in the fate of the Belgian Congo when it became the Democratic Republic of the Congo on 30 June 1960.

The run-up to independence was breathtaking. From its inception in 1908 the Belgian Congo had been run by decree from Brussels through a governor general in Léopoldville. The colony had no politicians, no political parties and no elections. No Congolese nor any Belgians residing in the Congo had a vote. But after World War II the winds of political change began to blow strongly, especially from those French ex-colonies which had already gained their independence, so that in 1956 Belgium was obliged to permit the formation of political parties in the Congo. By late1959 they had developed a momentum which culminated in a demand for speedy independence. Later that same year bloody riots erupted in Léopoldville in which hundreds were killed. This caused Belgium rapidly to rethink its colonial policy. In a state of near panic the Belgian government convened a round table conference in Brussels in February 1960 at which it resolved to grant the Congo immediate independence! Independence Day was to be 30 June 1960 – less than four months away.

In that short interval the Belgian government sought to instal a new Congolese government which would have a nationalistic character. Their expectation was that a unitary system of government, rather than one based on tribal affiliations, would allow Belgium the continued control of its ex-colony. To this end they favoured Patrice Lumumba, the leader of the only party with a nationalistic policy. All the other parties preferred a federal style constitution which they claimed would take into account the disparate elements existing in the Congo, its 225 tribes, for instance, and their desire for regional autonomy. But Lumumba won the general election and was called upon to form the first government of the Democratic Republic of the Congo with himself as prime minister.

Within four days of independence the Congolese army mutinied, running riot in an orgy of rape and looting. Chaos had come again. As though to pour petrol on the flames, Lumumba declared that Belgian army officers were responsible for the mutiny and that Belgium was plotting to reannex the Congo! This resulted in a mass exodus of Europeans. One of the scenes I recall vividly from those days was the sight of 600 stretcher cases, mostly Belgian women, lying in the hangars at Ndjili airport awaiting evacuation by air to Brussels.

Further rioting ensued, after which Belgium decided to send in paratroops to protect its nationals. Meanwhile, one thousand miles away in Élisabethville, the capital of Katanga province, Mr Moise Tshombe declared Katanga an independent sovereign state. However, the Independent State of Katanga failed to find official recognition in any foreign country then, or at any time thereafter, during the three years of its existence.

Mr Tshombe's first acts were to expel the mutinous elements of the Force Publique and to raise his own force of *gendarmerie*. (At a later stage my unit, 4 Commando, formed part of it.) The *gendarmerie* were used at once to put down a revolt by the 600,000 Baluba tribesmen who lived in northern Katanga. They had demanded their own independent state.

On 12 July Lumumba asked the UN to send military aid to the Congo to expel the Belgian 'forces of aggression' and to compel Katanga to end its secession. Three days later UN troops began to arrive, the advance guard of a corps which ultimately mustered over 25,000 men. Their task accomplished, the Belgian soldiers went. Lumumba declared martial law.

The Congo then began rapidly to disintegrate, politically. The people of the lower Congo, represented by ABAKO, the second largest political party, now demanded the abolition of the central government in favour of a confederation of independent provincial governments. This was followed by a declaration of independence by the State of Kasai headed by Albert Kalonji, who proclaimed himself 'King Albert' at the same time. Lumumba reacted violently to these threats at fragmentation, urging the UN to use their troops to reunify the country by force. They refused. Lumumba countered by appealing to the Soviet Union for military aid for this very purpose. They obliged. In mid-September nineteen Illyushin transport planes arrived in Léopoldville from Moscow with sufficient arms and transport to enable Lumumba to march on Kasai. In the one-sided battle which followed Lumumba's forces massacred the Kasai tribesmen in their hundreds. Flushed with this victory they then advanced on Katanga only to be repelled at the border.

But by this time Lumumba had shot his bolt. Although by all accounts a spellbinding demagogue, he had proved himself unstable as a diplomat and incompetent as head of government. President Kasavubu dismissed him from office. Lumumba dismissed the president. Kasavubu trumped his ace by placing him under house arrest. In the ensuing confusion the Communist members of the government withdrew to Stanleyville and set up their own independent regime under Antoine Gizenga.

The administration ground steadily to a halt. To save the country from total anarchy, Joseph Mobutu, a young colonel in the Congolese army, formed a college of administrators and took over the day-to-day running of the government. One of his first actions was to close the Soviet and Czech embassies and expel their members from the Congo.

Quiet reigned, but not for long. In January 1961 Lumumba escaped from house arrest intent on reaching Stanleyville, only to be captured *en route*. Kasavubu and Mobutu then sent him under armed guard to Élisabethville, where he was reluctantly received by Tshombe, apparently in a near-death condition. The following month the Katanga government announced that Lumumba had been killed while trying to escape from a mud hut in which he had been held prisoner. Furore broke out world-wide, Lumumba was declared a martyr in Communist circles and Tshombe's government held responsible for his murder.

Up till this time the UN forces in the Congo had been leading a somewhat gentlemanly existence, their ill defined but passive role being, apparently, to come between the assailants without actually involving themselves in anything unseemly. Apart from their being pleasantly ineffectual, the general impression they gave to the world at large was of an unsuccessful second eleven playing away from home. But back in Turtle Bay, UN Headquarters was about to change all that. On 21 February the Security Council, deeply concerned by the death of Lumumba and 'the danger of widespread civil war and bloodshed and the threat to international peace and security', passed a resolution which demanded, *inter alia*, 'the immediate withdrawal and evacuation from the Congo of all Belgian and other foreign military and paramilitary personnel and political advisers not under the UN command and mercenaries'.

Moise Tshombe reacted at once by calling an all-party conference in Tananarive, Mozambique, which roundly rejected the UN Security Council resolution of 21 February, demanded the immediate withdrawal of UN troops from the Congo and declared in favour of a confederal constitution. The repercussions in New York to this spirited initiative by Tshombe were instant and far-reaching. It decided on the morrow to take some positive action against Katanga which would force it to submit to Leo. The United States came out strongly in favour of this policy, thereby influencing Third World countries decisively in favour of the UN's proposed action. With the benefit of hindsight it seems to me that this was the precise moment when the balance was weighed against Mr Tshombe. From then on, you could say he was fighting world opinion, uninformed to a large extent perhaps but in the end conclusive.

As the result of feverish activity behind the scenes in New York, Kasavubu was persuaded to accept the UN resolution of 21 February. In return, it was generally supposed, the

Congo was promised considerable financial aid. In this submissive mood Kasavubu agreed to repudiate the Tananarive agreement.

This left Tshombe out on a limb. He called a new conference to be held near Coquilhatville to consider the turn of events. He began, unwisely but truthfully, by denouncing the president, saying that Kasavubu had betrayed him by repudiating the resolutions agreed upon at the Tananarive conference. This resulted in his immediate imprisonment. It took the form of house arrest on an island in the Congo river and lasted for two months.

Early June of that year saw the installation of yet another new government, this time under Cyrille Adoulla, which included Gbenye and Gizenga, the Communist members from the breakaway province of Oriental. An influx of foreign Communists followed, together with the immediate return of the Soviet and Czech embassies to the capital.

At the end of August Mr Conor Cruise O'Brien, the UN representative in Katanga, issued an ultimatum to Tshombe to submit to the central government in Léopoldville and implement the resolution of 21 February. The ultimatum was rejected by the Katangese. The UN then decided to use force. This culminated in the expulsion of a number of foreign political advisers from Katanga and, among other things of relatively minor importance, the disbandment of 4 Commando, the mercenary unit of which I was commander.

But the impasse continued. In an attempt to resolve matters on the ground, Mr Dag Hammarskjöld, the Secretary General of the United Nations, decided to fly to Katanga for a personal meeting with Mr Tshombe. On 17 September, as his plane made its final approach to Ndola airport in Northern Rhodesia, it crashed into some trees, killing everybody on board.

Thus passed the last reasonable chance at mediation between the central government and the Independent State of Katanga. Force was now presumed to be the only option left to the United Nations. Early in December 1961 they decided to use their troops, supported by bomber and fighter aircraft, to attack Katanga. This decision signalled a fundamental switch in UN policy from passive peace-keeping to active intervention. Their operation succeeded but their very success forced the dove of peace to fly the UN coop, never to return in the Congo. Tshombe was then induced to sign an eight-point agreement with Cyrille Adoulla at Kitona under which he agreed to end Katanga's secession. Gizenga and Gbenye returned to Stanleyville to continue their separate existence.

The whole of 1962 dragged by with endless discussion on the terms of the Kitona agreement. Finally, convinced that Tshombe was merely stalling for time, the UN decided in December1962 to mount a full-scale invasion of Katanga to put an end to its secession once and for all. The outcome was the final overthrow of Mr Tshombe by force of arms. Blood was shed far and wide. The Independent State of Katanga ceased to exist. Mortified, the ex-president sought voluntary exile in Spain.

The state of play in the Congo could then be described as one down and one to go, the one to go being the separatist movement in Stanleyville which continued to defy the Léopoldville government. For reasons which I have never been able to fathom, the UN did not seem half as keen to force the reintegration of that Communist-run separatist state into the central government as they were to smash Tshombe. Nothing was done to end their secession.

Early in 1964 reports began to filter through to Léopoldville that a Communist-inspired revolution was in the making. It had its core in the Kwilu district of Léopoldville province. By May it had developed into a full-scale revolt. From Kwilu its epicentre moved to Stanleyville which now came out in armed rebellion against the Léopoldville government. The National Army in Oriental retreated westwards as quickly as it could, or joined the rebels. Within a month the rebel army, now calling themselves Simbas, lions, began their march on the capital, carrying everything before them. They appeared to be unstoppable. By the end of June they had captured the whole of Kivu province and occupied Albertville in Katanga. Two thirds of the country was now in their hands with their line of supply secure. It stretched down the Nile and across the Sudan into Aba in north eastern Congo, and from there to Paulis and Stanleyville. A further line of supply ran through Tanganyika, via Dar es Salaam and Kigoma, across the lake to Albertville.

Things were now extremely grave for the Léopoldville government. The rebels were advancing with the speed and

ferocity of a bush fire. In the face of the victorious rebels the
National Army had melted away, paralysed in many cases
by their belief in witchcraft as practised by the Simbas. By the
end of June their advanced elements were less than 160
kilometres from the capital. The politicians met to find a
solution. The most unexpected one was to invite Mr
Tshombe to return from his exile in Spain to become prime
minister of the Congo!

He returned to the country on the very day that the United
Nations pulled out of the Congo, 1 July 1964. At the same
time the rebels continued their inexorable advance on the
capital. The government had now no option but to take
desperate measures. In the middle of July, with the agreement of the Belgian and American governments, they decided to raise a force of mercenary soldiers to assist the
Congolese National Army in its life and death struggle
against the rebels. A few days later Alistair Wicks and I were
invited to visit Mr Tshombe, the new prime minister, in
Léopoldville. At a meeting of his security council, chaired by
the C-in-C, General Mobutu, I was asked to recruit a force of
one thousand mercenary soldiers to help the Armée
Nationale Congolaise put down the rebellion.

The story of the raising of this force, which I named 5
Commando, the stemming of the rebel advance at the eleventh hour, the subsequent march on Stanleyville to rescue
125 hostages held by the rebel regime, and the appalling
massacre which took place there at the hands of the rebels
on 24 November 1964, at the very moment when salvation
was at hand, is told in my book *Congo Mercenary*.

The stories in this book are all connected with the events
of those two years. Some are intended to be lightweight and,
I hope, fairly amusing; some are tragic, just as things were
in the Congo. But all shed some light on the events of the day
and on the life of a mercenary soldier.

Ten years after the Belgian Congo had become the Democratic Republic of the Congo, and later the Republic of Zaïre,
a large number of place-names were changed in order to
depict more accurately their indigenous origins.
Léopoldville became Kinshasa, Stanleyville became
Kisangani, Élisabethville became Lubumbashi, Albertville
became Kalémié, and so on. As the events described in this
book all took place in the years just after independence I have

retained the original colonial place-names which were in use at the time.

1

The Melody Lingers On

After fifty-two years as a Belgian colony, the Democratic Republic of the Congo came into existence on 30 June 1960. Eleven days later, alarmed at the anarchy and breakdown of law and order which had occurred in the rest of the Congo, Mr Tshombe declared Katanga a sovereign state, the Independent State of Katanga. This action was vigorously denounced by the Léopoldville government, the United Nations and numerous countries around the world, many of them Communist-inclined. But of more immediate importance to Mr Tshombe's new state at this time was the reaction of the 600,000 Baluba tribesmen who inhabited northern Katanga. They wanted to establish their own independent regime under their leader, Jason Sendwe, but were thwarted when they narrowly lost a vote on the resolution in the Katangese parliament. The Baluba then came out in open rebellion against the Independent State of Katanga and with primitive arms, plus a number of modern weapons, crossed the Luvua river, captured the tin-mining town of Manono and began a march on Élisabethville.

Fortunately for Mr Tshombe, he had taken the precaution of raising his own force of *gendarmerie* shortly after declaring Katanga independent, so that he was able to offer resistance and ultimately to quell the rebellion. It was in these circumstances that I first served as a mercenary soldier as part of Mr. Tshombe's *gendarmerie*. I was given command of a unit of mercenary soldiers, made up from nineteen different nationalities, which I called '4 Commando'.

It was during this campaign against the Baluba that the Belgian officers who had served in the Force Publique, the colonial army of the Belgian Congo, saw fit to warn me:

'Watch out! It's not the enemy – it's the bloody country that will get you!' I hadn't been in the Katanga long before I realized the truth of that remark.

Nature was at its most spectacular in this part of Africa. When the sun shone on the high plateau which is Katanga, it burned your skin within minutes. When the rain fell, it soaked you, flooding the roads and tracks. Everything grew in amazing profusion. A paved road, if left for a year unattended, would disappear altogether under the virulent growth. Powerful roots would overrun the tarmac, force it up from below, crack the surface and then wait for the rains to do the rest. In the flooded ditches which lay alongside some of the massive Congolese rivers, giant misshapen mushrooms lay side by side with orchids of an unbelievable beauty.

But there was little time to stand and stare. In these watery conditions malaria was endemic. And in the bush un-diagnosable fevers could be transmitted to us via small bugs picked up as we pushed our way through the high grass or through the tangled undergrowth of knotted lianas. Astro-nomically high body temperatures were the result. In the heat of the noonday sun a minor gunshot wound stood a good chance of turning gangrenous within hours unless immediate medical attention was on hand. Field first aid, usually with amateurishly applied tourniquets, often has-tened the onset of gangrene, resulting in the amputation of limbs and sometimes in death. Such were the perils of sol-diering in this country. The Belgians were right: it was the country which would get you. The enemy were insignificant by comparison.

My unit, 4 Commando, had been ordered to escort fifty brand-new five-ton trucks from Élisabethville, the capital, to a place in northern Katanga called Nyunzu, an important railhead about half-way between Albertville on the shores of Lake Tanganyika and Kabalo, a port on the mighty Lualaba river. The freight consisted of much-needed stores for the Katangese garrisons in the north, ranging from ammunition to American C-rations, hundred-kilogram sacks of rice, evil-smelling dried fish and bales of manioc, the staple diet of the Katangese. The journey would be about 1,350 kilometres and in normal circumstances should take no more than four or five days. But the gilded staff who had planned the operation had not reckoned with the problems of the country.

After eleven days we had barely reached the half-way point and were bogged down on the sodden track which disintegrated after the passage of the first ten trucks. Worse still, we were now surrounded by an unseen Baluba enemy whose reputation as ruthless and cruel fighters had gone out before them. The Katangese soldiers, mostly from the Lunda tribe, needed no reminder of the methods employed in warfare by their traditional enemy the Baluba. Prisoners of war would be killed after ritual torture. It was an age-old custom. It didn't bear thinking about. So that now that the going was getting rougher by the hour, the morale of the Katangese drivers began to crack and many of them deserted. In some cases they deliberately drove their trucks into the ditches, which gave them a chance to broach their cargoes and drink themselves paralytic drunk.

We clawed our way northward, miserable kilometre by miserable kilometre. The route lay first toward Baudouinville and then Kapona, which I knew was fairly open country at a higher altitude, and therefore in all probability more favourable to the passage of our convoy. Our progress was pitiful. In one day we notched up a mere fifteen kilometres, the whole day going in road-making and unditching. The rain came down relentlessly, day and night, drenching every man to the skin. The track disintegrated completely and in places was no better than a stream of water. I considered the wisdom of calling a two-day halt for maintenance and rest. Perhaps that would also give the road a chance to dry out. If only we could have had four hours of sunshine, the track would be passable again. That I knew from experience in Africa is the general rule anywhere south of the equator. But the wretched sun never showed.

The men of 4 Commando were exhausted, totally demoralized, sodden with the continuous rain and bloodyminded. In many cases they looked as though they might be going down with malaria. Two bright sparks had contracted a spectacular species of gonorrhea which had defied the medicos, and it was four weeks since any mail had been distributed. All the makings of discontent were present. I discussed our situation with Stan Dowsey, my sergeant major, and asked him how much more of this he thought the men could take.

'Got to give them a proper rest, sir. No good going on like this day after day. They're going to crack up pretty soon, and then Gawd knows what will happen.'

He was right. To press the men further would certainly have ended in disaster. I examined the map. Eight kilometres down the track was a Katangese outpost. Twenty-five kilometres beyond that was a small town in no man's land. That dot meant there was an inn there. I figured that if we could make the outpost in another day I could persuade the *commandant de place* to guard the column for twenty-four hours while we, the escort, pressed on for the inn, where we could have a rest and a clean-up. The prospect of a whole day's break would work wonders. If the men were told the plan, they would perk up at once. From headquarters' point of view I imagined it would probably be seen very differently, but I decided to risk it.

Two days later, at about ten o'clock at night in blinding rain, my jeep slithered to a halt outside a double-storeyed building in a desolate village. Some faded red lettering on the wall above the bolted door proclaimed that this was the 'Auberge de la Forêt'. There was no sign of life.

'Do your stuff, Stan,' I said.

Stan hammered on the door with the butt end of his Browning pistol, the rain cascading down his groundsheet, soaking his knees. There was no reply.

'Try again, Stan.'

The rest of the column closed right up, fender to fender, motors ticking over steadily as we waited, the jeep headlights throwing a milky glare into the vertical rainfall. The windows of the inn were shuttered, Mediterranean-style, and everything looked bolted and barred. '*Fin de saison!*' said one of my more sophisticated types. Damn it, just our flaming luck! I began to wonder if the place had been abandoned. It wouldn't have surprised me if it had. Suddenly a light flickered in a room on the first floor. That was better. Somebody was coming down the stairs. The heavy front door creaked open cautiously and checked against a security chain. Stan spoke in muffled tones to a figure behind the door. He turned and laughed.

'OK, sir. *Bienvenue!*' Stan loved to think he could speak French.

The men began to dismount and stretched themselves after the long ride. I went inside to explain who we were and what we wanted. The Belgian *patron*, an ancient *colon*, thought nothing of opening the inn at this hour of night to soldiers, but madame, tight-lipped in dressing-gown and mobcap, hovered anxiously in the background wringing her hands in despair. She was *désolée*.

'*Pas de nourriture!*' she moaned.

'What's that all about, sir?' asked Stan.

'No grub, Sergeant Major.'

I asked her if there was anything to drink, and she said yes, there was, plenty. That suited us. We were long past hunger but a few beers would go down nicely. Could we doss down on the verandas? Yes, of course, and they had some fresh straw in the stable. Lovely. But sorry again, there was nothing to eat.

'San fairy anne,' said Stan. (His father was in France during the Great War and had bequeathed him these anglicized pearls from the language of love.) 'Who wants to eat in the middle of the night anyway?'

'Belgians!' somebody said.

Simba beer there was by the crate, pastis and whisky galore. The men filled the bar, shedding their dripping groundsheets in the passage outside. When all the chairs were taken, they sat on the floor with their backs against the walls, dampness oozing out of their clammy uniforms. Soon the place was jam-packed, lit by the warm glow of two or three paraffin lamps. The Belgian proprietors looked at us and each other with mounting dismay. They didn't like the look of the weapons for a start. Would we pay? And what might liquor do to us? Apprehension and alarm were written all over their faces. I put my arm round the *patron*'s shoulders to reassure him. He was a good old chap. If they were kind enough to open the place for us, I told him, he had my assurance we would behave. I hoped I wouldn't have to eat my words; one never knew with some of these types. The old pair retreated behind the counter defensively and began to serve the men.

After the first few drinks had been downed, a happy hubbub of conversation and laughter filled the room. This was more like it. The accumulated tensions and frustrations of the last fourteen days began to ebb slowly away, and finally to evaporate in that warm spirit of camaraderie known especially to soldiers who have faced common hardship and danger. It was, if you had stopped to think about it, a memorable moment.

Then it was time for a song. Stan got to his feet and rendered – his own expression – an old favourite loved by one and all, 'Maybe it's because I'm a Londoner.' Stan had a ripe cockney tenor, trained, he once told me with pride and a hint of nostalgia, outside some of the best public houses in the Old Kent Road. Many the tanner he'd earned with a tearjerker when he was a nipper, he said, in his native Kennington. He began. The men quieted down. He put the heartbreak in the right places and led the chorus, announcing the next line ahead of time in the best sing-along fashion. He got a big hand. Stan was a disciplinarian but had the maturity that came from much experience in the handling of men. A rare gift. At a time like this he knew how to take their backchat and ribald remarks without offence, pretty confident that when they were on parade again they would not take advantage.

'Song!' they all shouted, and an aspirant Mario Lanza obliged with deep breaths, much clearing of the throat and eventually something from *The Student Prince*. 'Overhead the moon is shining,' he began. But like the moon it was much too high. This earned him the bird amid some good-natured barracking.' "Back to Sorrento", Mario', Stan advised. 'Safer, that one, mate.'

The patron was smiling now. He whispered to his wife. 'Don't worry, *chérie*. Everything's going to be all right, just like I said.'

But madame was still a little nervous. You never knew with *les anglais*: they had such extraordinary drinking habits. She hoped there were no *irlandais* among them. She shuddered. 'You remember that time ... just after the war in Brussels, Maurice ... yes, you do, VE day in the Place de la Ville, that man with the red hair ... he was *irlandais* ... of course you remember ... *nom de Dieu*, how could anyone ever forget?' She shivered at the thought, and that had happened years ago.

We had been there more than an hour. The atmosphere was warm and cosy and smoke-laden. Suddenly the conversation ebbed into almost complete silence for no particular

reason. Seamus Patrick Kelly shambled to his feet. He was
an awkward sort of customer, and nature hadn't been particularly kind to him in the looks department. He was a
Scouse, a Liverpool Irishman from the Scotland Road. A
failed civilian and an untidy mess as a soldier. For many good
reasons he was the most unpopular man in the unit. The
South Africans could not understand what he was saying
half the time, and the continentals did not trust him. He had
taking ways, they said, the unforgivable sin in barracks.
Kelly took a swig of beer and began to sing. Nobody paid any
attention to him, just went on talking. Drinks were passed
across him as he was singing – not deliberately, it was just
that he didn't amount to much. But it didn't seem right to
Stan. He called for a proper hearing, casting himself in the
role of Chairman of the Palace of Varieties for the occasion.

'Fair dos, you blokes. Give the singer a chance. Come on
now, lads – ta ra! ra ra! ra ra! – I give you, Volunteer Kelly!'

Most of the chatter died down. Kelly began again, stronger
this time and with a little more confidence. Now we listened.
I seemed to know that tune, sounded familiar, what was it,
yes, hadn't heard that one in years. 'Gentlemen rankers out
on the spree.' That was it. One of Bing Crosby's. Bit of
Kipling, wasn't it? Kelly's voice was coarse but quite tuneful.
You could tell he'd done a bit of singing in his time. No
gimmicks, just straight from the heart. Gradually the talking
stopped as Kelly's voice filled the smoky room. Then he
swung into the chorus. One or two men with good voices
picked up the refrain and began to harmonize with him.

> We're poor little lambs who've lost our way,
> Baa, baa, baa.
> We're little black sheep who've gone astray,
> Baa, baa, baa.

And then the rest of us joined in, good voices and bad
voices, all together, swelling the chorus with an indefinable
pathos.

> Gentlemen rankers out on the spree,
> Damned from here to eternity,
> God have mercy on such as we,
> Baa, baa, baa.

He sat down. There was no clapping and no laughter. Just an awkward silence. Kelly had put into words something nobody really wanted to hear. Soldiers of fortune. Loners. Many of us rootless. Far from home and loved ones – if any. God have mercy on such as we. Perhaps that was right; perhaps we were damned from here to eternity. One or two men stirred uneasily to hide their embarrassment. A barrage of swearing broke out, the subterfuge strong men resort to when they find themselves in an awkward situation. Somebody called for a round of drinks, and the spell was broken.

Now Stan was waving to me from the other side of the room and pointing to his watch. It was one in the morning. I decided to let it go on for a bit longer. The therapy was worth $10 a minute. I left quietly, unobserved, as the mood clawed its way back to its former cheerfulness. Kelly and his song were forgotten, but something lingered on, damn him.

I lay on my bed and heard the songs again in the distance, bawdy and sentimental, cheerful and sad, coming and going on the wet night air. But at three in the morning all was quiet save for the pacing of the sentry outside my door, the crunch of gravel under his boots, and the comforting pitter-patter of rain on the iron roof above my head.

Reprinted by permission of the publisher from *The Road to Kalamata* by Mike Hoare (Lexington, Mass.: Lexington Books, D.C. Heath and Company, © 1989 Mike Hoare).

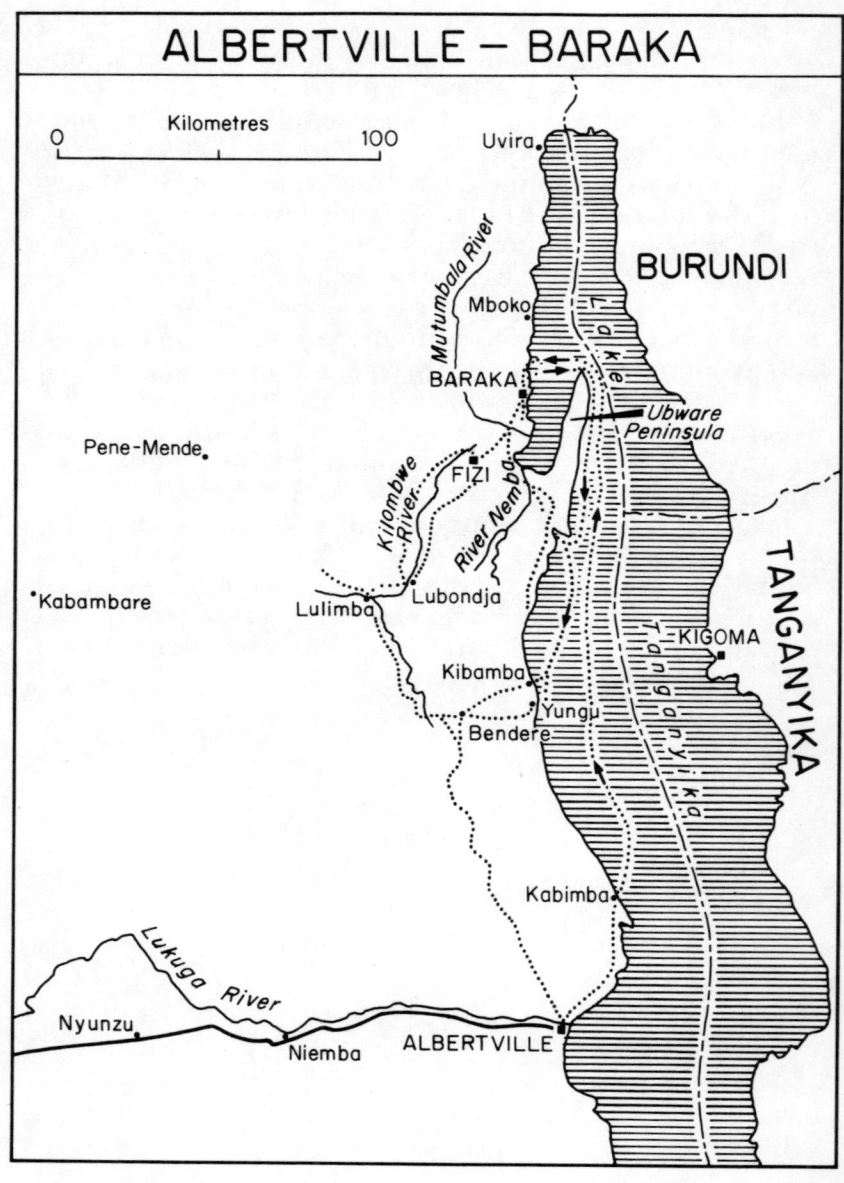

ALBERTVILLE — BARAKA

Kilometres

0   100

Uvira

BURUNDI

Mutumbala River

Mboko

Lake

BARAKA

Ubware
Peninsula

Pene-Mende

Kilombwe River

FIZI

River Nemba

Tanganyika

KIGOMA

Kabambare

Lulimba

Lubondja

Kibamba

Yungu

TANGANYIKA

Bendere

Kabimba

Lukuga River

Nyunzu

Niemba

ALBERTVILLE

2

The Fortress at Yungu

Tom Harrison was about forty-eight years of age when I first met him. He had just sailed across the Indian Ocean from Australia, via New Guinea, in his twenty-five-foot sloop named *Sundowner*, single handed. The damned thing was so tender you had to part your hair in the middle if you didn't want it to heel. Tom, who was a master carpenter, had built her himself back in Australia and rigged her with a lug sail. He reckoned that would make her easier to handle than the usual Bermuda rig and might be better for extended single-handed cruising. He was probably right.

On the way over from Port Moresby, Tom had made two prolonged stops, one at the Cocos Keeling Islands and the other at Réunion Island. Later, on his way over to Durban, he had weathered a cyclone in the Mozambique Channel which had lasted over sixty hours, and blown him 300 kilometres off his course. Tom didn't regard that as anything very unusual. He just hove-to and rode it out, everything battened down. When he finally sailed into Durban harbour, he was given a berth at Bayhead alongside my thirty-six-foot gaff-rigged cutter *Colin Archer*, and that's how we came to be firm friends.

Tom was the archetype Australian bushwhacker. He hated any form of pretence, socializing, fancy restaurants, posh talk, dressing up and unnecessary regulations. Yacht clubs and cocktail parties were anathema to him. He loved the bush, the loneliness of the sea (but not the sea itself, for which he had a wholesome respect) good solid tucker and the occasional booze-up with old mates. He thought of himself as a very ordinary guy.

He had served in an Australian infantry regiment during

the war and taken part in what must have been one of the roughest and toughest campaigns ever to have been fought by any army anywhere – the crossing of the Owen Stanley mountain range from Port Moresby to Morobe. So that when 5 Commando was mustering at Kamina, a military base in the Katanga province of the Congo, I was not surprised to find Tom turn up in one of the early intakes. I made him a sergeant at once.

We were a battalion of mercenary soldiers created by order of Prime Minister Moise Tshombe and Major-General Joseph Désiré Mobutu of the Democratic Republic of the Congo. Our primary purpose was to assist the Congolese National Army in putting down a Communist-inspired rebellion which had broken out in the north-eastern corner of the Congo. It had spread across the country with the speed and ferocity of a bush fire, so that now, three months later, the rebel army, the Armée Populaire de Libération, was within eighty kilometres of the capital, Léopoldville.

We were to be the spearhead of a 4,000-man mechanized brigade, under the command of a Belgian brigadier. His intention was to march on Stanleyville, some 1,500 kilometres away, and liberate the 125 white hostages being held prisoner by the rebels. Another 250 were being held at Paulis, a city some 400 kilometres north-east of it. Training for this task had begun.

The youngsters in his commando did not take to Tom. He was too old, they reckoned, overlooking the fact that he could have outlasted the lot of them on a march or on a cross-country trek through the bush. But when our training period was over and it came to moving out of barracks and into the field, they found out the relative importance of those things and welcomed him with open arms. Then he began to teach them how to survive through bushcraft, how to live off the land, how to make a cross country march by compass, how to navigate by the sun and the stars, how to read the directional signs nature gives us on trees and ant hills, how to exist when isolated. Then they respected him. But they never got to love him. I don't think anybody ever did. I knew him better than most and couldn't find the way in: his shell was almost impregnable.

I soon made full use of his special talents. Tom understood rivers, currents and sand bars. His experience of these conditions in New Guinea made him invaluable to me in the Congo, which is plagued in the same way with fast-running rivers – plagued, that is, from an infantryman's point of view. Faced with these problems I would send for Tom. And whenever he was on the water, at the wheel of a tug or a ferry, I would relax my strict rules against fancy dress, which I loathed, and allow him to wear his captain's yachting cap. Just a little distinction in which he took a great pride.

It was 24 November 1964. After a gruelling 1,500 kilometre approach march, 5 Commando, at the head of a mechanized brigade, entered Stanleyville just after dawn to free 125 white hostages held by the rebels for the past 111 days. But we were too late. We found thirty of the hostages brutally murdered in an insane act of revenge. Among them was an American missionary doctor, Paul Carlson, killed by a single bullet through the head as he made a last-minute bid to escape over a low wall.

By early the next day the action was over and we were in full control of the commercial part of the city and its docks. I made my way down to the Otraco Beach, the shipping wharf at the river's edge. It was my first sight of the Congo river proper. The mighty stream, over a kilometre and a half wide at this point, was flowing steadily at about three knots, carrying everything before it in a rush of muddy brown water, half-submerged trees, reeds, bushes, even small islands of papyrus. Half way across the river some fishing nets, strung between a line of bamboo poles, strained against the current. One or two dug-out canoes were made fast to the poles, and fishermen stood in their pirogues spearing the fish just as they had since time immemorial. The tragedy which had taken place the day before meant nothing to them. Close by were the famous Stanley Falls which marked the limit of navigation upstream. From here the river flowed unhindered all the way down to Kinshasa, 1,600 kilometres away, where navigation ceased at Stanley Pool.

I stood on the wooden wharf, looking across at the left bank. On the other side the rebels were holding more hostages, including an entire Roman Catholic mission. If the priests were to escape with their lives, a rescue party must get across to them at once: there was not a minute to lose. I sent for Tom.

The only ship which looked as though it might be big and strong enough to carry an assault group was a small tug named *Geri*, a ship of about eighty tons. Tom shinned down an iron ladder into the engine-room. If he could get the engine going, he said, we could put a hundred men on board in a matter of minutes and storm the other side. But even if he could, Tom reckoned the tug was too big for him to handle on his own. Furthermore he would definitely need some local knowledge of the river and the sandbanks. But were there any charts? Could we find the ship's crew?

The ship's watchman told him the two men who made up the normal crew were hiding in the *cité*, the rabbit warren of huts and shacks spread over two or three square miles, where the local people lived. If we could reach them, he was sure they would come. OK then, could he show us the way? He could.

Tom decided to go into the *cité* and get hold of the crew himself. He reckoned a quick dash in and out would probably be safer than the full-scale fighting patrol which I suggested. In less than five minutes he had readied a jeep for the trip, removed the windshield and covered the hood with sandbags. He mounted a MAG machine-gun on the top of the pile and hung a spare cartridge belt of 200 rounds around his chest. He wore his yachtsman's cap. I was in two minds about letting him go, as the rebels were everywhere. It seemed to me his chances of finding the crew were slim to begin with, and of bringing them back alive even slimmer. But Tom reckoned it was worth a shot. Once more he refused an escort or any more men to travel with him in the jeep. Better to rely on speed, he reckoned, quick in and quick out. He roared off up the hill, throwing me a salute of sorts. Tom was no regimental soldier. Meanwhile I ordered the hundred-man assault party to assemble.

An hour later Tom returned. His jeep had been ambushed on the way back. There were three Congolese in the vehicle. Two of them were wearing the white headbands which would distinguish them from the rebels, in accordance with an edict from HQ. They were the crew of the *Geri*. A third Congolese was lying dead on the floor, a bullet through his head. He was the ship's watchman. Dammit. The death of their mate seemed to have little effect on the other two. Perhaps they had seen too much violence in the last few weeks, poor devils. Tom had a bullet wound in the calf of his right leg, which was bleeding profusely. We gave him some tea while we got it bandaged up and stopped the flow of blood. He said he was all right.

The crew jumped on board and in less than fifteen minutes I heard the comforting sound of the powerful diesel engines, bidoom, bidoom, bidoom, and felt the vibration of the tug as she came alive. As soon as my troops, commanded by Captain Ian Gordon, had embarked, Tom pulled out for the other bank with a farewell blast on his siren.

Just before sundown the tug returned. We had had no radio contact with the assault party since they left. I focused my binoculars on them when they were still only half-way across. I could see the foredeck quite clearly. It was piled high with what looked like dirty white clothing. That's just what it was. As the tug came nearer, I could see the bodies of thirty-two dead priests piled high, one on top of another, in grotesque positions, on the foredeck. Tom was at the wheel. He opened the door of the wheelhouse and hailed me through a megaphone.

'Sorry, Major. We were too late!'

But he had brought back an Englishwoman and her two young daughters who had hidden under a staircase while the massacre had taken place, and released a large number of black nuns from a nearby convent. These were all safe on board. I detailed some men to escort them to a reception centre for the wounded and homeless where they would be properly cared for.

We buried the priests in Stanleyville cemetery the next day.

The contract ended five weeks later and Tom returned to Durban and *Sundowner*. When he had started out from New Guinea, his intention was to sail round the world single handed. Time was not a consideration. He would maintain himself by working at his trade as and when he needed to. The Congo had just been an adventurous episode on the way. Now he would use some of the money he had made as a mercenary soldier to overhaul his ship.

I visited Tom during the two weeks leave I had been granted in January 1965. The two of us went for a three-day cruise offshore in my ship *Colin Archer*, when Tom taught me some more of the art of sailing. 'Never beat!' was the rule he cruised by. 'Sailing boats, particularly heavy jobs like this one, are meant to be pushed from behind, not pulled. Go 300 kilometres out of your way with a following wind, or at worst one abeam, rather than beat eighty kilometres.' The wisdom of the ages. Stanleyville could have been a place on the moon for all it meant to us.

Tom's leg wound had healed perfectly and as he had already received compensation for it, there was nothing to stop him sailing away, other than the proposed refit of *Sundowner*. But he would have to work fast if he wanted to sail by the end of February, which is normally the end of the sailing season for the trade-wind voyage to South America from the Cape via St Helena.

I returned to the Congo and completed another contract.

At the start of the third contract 5 Commando was based in Albertville, on Lake Tanganyika.

The famous rift valley of Africa, one of the world's outstanding geographic faults, stretches from the eastern Mediterranean down the length of the Nile, and beyond, for over 5,000 kilometres, to end in Lake Nyasa. It creates, in succession, the great central African lakes of Albert, Edward, Kivu and Tanganyika. In addition, to the east of Edward and Kivu is Lake Victoria, bigger than all of them all put together, a lake the size of an inland sea, and the source of the White Nile.

Lake Tanganyika itself is a massive cleft in the earth's surface that stretches due north and south for a distance of over 640 kilometres, from Burundi in the north to Zambia in the south, having Tanganyika on its east coast and the Congo on its west. The lake is seventy kilometres wide at its widest point and averages fifty for most of its length.

Albertville, where we were now stationed, is about halfway down the lake on its western side. The only major town on the eastern side is Kigoma, the terminus of the railway line from Dar es Salaam, the capital of Tanganyika. Kigoma is about 150 kilometres across the lake from Albertville in a north-easterly direction. From our point of view, the fact that Kigoma was almost immediately opposite the rebel-held lakeside towns of Baraka and Yungu on the Congo side made it of great strategic importance.

With the successful completion of our campaign in the Oriental province of the Congo, the inflow of arms and supplies to the rebels down the Nile and across the Congo-Sudan borders at Aba and Faradje had all but ceased. The flow of arms and ammunition which had been channelled via Uganda through the twin towns of Aru and Arua, one on each side of the border, had also dwindled to a trickle. Now the rebels' only remaining line of supply was via Tanganyika, from Dar es Salaam to Kigoma by rail, and then across the lake by a multitude of small craft ranging from twelve-foot boats to fifty-foot cabin cruisers, sailing dhows and self-propelled barges.

The inflow of arms and equipment to the rebels was estimated by GHQ in Léopoldville to exceed more than thirty tons per day. For the rebels it was a relatively short haul across the lake. The total distance from Kigoma to Baraka was only 160 kilometres, the first half of it within Tanganyikan territorial waters, so that the other half could easily be completed under cover of darkness. To Yungu it was very much less.

It was now known that a contingent of one hundred Cuban mercenary soldiers had arrived from Cuba via Tanganyika, to stiffen up the opposition. They were reputed to be under the leadership of Che Guevara, lately one of Fidel Castro's lieutenants. Their headquarters was situated in the almost impregnable fortress of Yungu, the small port 120 kilometres north of Albertville, half way to Baraka. The terrain behind the port and to the north of it was ideally suited to guerrilla warfare. It was for the most part mountainous and well forested, with very few roads. Baraka and Fizi were the major towns held by the rebels.

GHQ had indicated that the most pressing need in this campaign was interdiction – in other words, to stop the supply of military hardware reaching the rebels from across the lake. For this they would provide me with a navy. And in due course I was given an eighty-foot merchant ship named *Ermans* for use as a gun boat, and six PT boats for patrolling the lake. These were specially flown in by C130 from the United States. Later I was to get another five Swifts, bigger, faster and better than the PT boats in every way.

The navy comprised forty men from 5 Commando, all volunteers, some of whom had been sailors before. But it was too important a unit, with too important a role, to leave in the hands of amateurs. I needed someone to command it who

understood the limitations of fresh-water craft, their maintenance and their tactical handling. The obvious man was Tom
Harrison. I sent him a telegram care of the port captain's
office, Durban, and two weeks later was delighted when he
walked into my office in Albertville. I offered him the ap-
pointment, with the rank of captain. He leapt at it. Fortunately for me, he had not made his February deadline and
had been obliged to postpone his trip to South America until
November, when the south-east trades would be right for
him once more.

He began by training his men. Then he organized patrols
in the PT boats to interdict the supplies coming across the lake
from Kigoma. Finally he converted *Ermans* into a gunboat,
whose most formidable armament was a 57 mm recoilless
rifle, mounted in the bows. This weapon is really a small
cannon, despite its misleading name, and the smaller brother
of the awe-inspiring 75 mm recoilless rifle, the so called *canon
sans recul*, which is a much better name for the gun, telling
you exactly what it is – namely, a cannon that has no recoil. I
believe it was invented by a Frenchman, so, not surprisingly,
it had to have a bore of 75 mm.

This artillery piece is a comparatively recent invention in
the world of ordnance and unique in that it operates on the
principle that the explosion which causes the forward thrust
of the projectile can be made equal to its backward thrust. If
louvres or vents are built into the after portion of the breech,
to allow for the escape of most of this backward thrust, the
weapon will have no recoil but will still have enough power
to propel a 75 mm diameter shell eight kilometres or more,
with a fairly flat trajectory. It works beautifully in practice.
The only snag is that the backward blast is fierce enough to
kill anybody who might stand close up behind the gun when
it is fired.

But apart from the forward and backward blast there is a
third force which must travel down its tripod and mounting,
a force which would be more or less at right angles to the
barrel.

Tom and I discussed the nature of this third force at length.
We appreciated, from an elementary study of the parallelogram of forces, that the downward force must be considerable. On solid ground it would be absorbed by solid earth, we
assumed, and so would be of little consequence. But when

mounted on a ship its downward thrust would have to be reckoned with. How would it dissipate itself? What damage might it do? We never came to a satisfactory conclusion but decided in the end that, as the deck on *Ermans* below the 57 mm cannon, was strong enough to sustain the downward thrust, all would be well. And so it proved.

In due course Tom led his little flotilla out on raids as far as Baraka on our side of the lake and Kigoma on the other, disregarding the international boundary which runs down the centre of the lake and separates Tanganyika from the Congo. Tom always claimed he couldn't see any dotted lines on the water, so could never say for sure which country he was in.

Very soon the PT boats began to intercept all manner of craft, dhows and barges, even papyrus rafts, carrying supplies across to Baraka and Yungu and the Ubware peninsula, a finger of land jutting out from the mainland south of Baraka, to form Burton Bay. Prisoners were taken from time to time, including two Cubans, from whom we learned details of the strength and disposition of their contingent at Yungu. They confirmed that Che Guevara was leading them. Meanwhile Tom's navy was doing exceptionally well. The supply of arms to the rebels was dwindling, and the general was delighted with his navy and its performance.

The PT boat is a marvel of naval construction. It is about twenty-five feet long with a seven-foot beam. It is capable of over twenty knots in a calm sea. It has a draft of less than two inches and is propelled by a jet or jets of water emitted from the stern. These jets are in every way superior to the normal screw. For one thing they are completely silent; for another there is nothing to get enmeshed in seaweed or grass. It is thus the ideal craft to use when a stealthy approach to the land is required.

This was my special and urgent need right now. My overall plan for the campaign was to land a considerable amphibious force some weeks later on a beach, or beaches, north of Baraka, and to capture the stronghold by surprise from the lake. If we were successful, this victory would shorten the war by several months. Detailed reconnaissance of those beaches was therefore my priority.

I asked Tom to arrange a rehearsal just for the two of us. We would sail up the lake in *Ermans* and when about eight kilometres off Baraka he and I would transfer to a PT boat to make a preliminary recce of suitable landing beaches. This would have to be done on a night when there was no moon. Fortunately the PT boats were equipped with radar, effective to about eleven kilometres. The screen gave the shape of the coast in some detail and made it possible to identify certain beaches on our charts with ease.

I joined Tom on the deck of *Ermans* in Albertville just before midnight. It was a dark and cloudy night. We pushed off for Baraka, about 240 kilometres north of us, attended by the fussy little flotilla of PT boats. *Ermans* was capable of a respectable eight knots without strain, so that after a day's steaming we were within striking distance of Baraka. Again it was a pitch-black night. All our lights were doused. We closed with the shore and anchored off, now about five kilometres from the coast.

Just after midnight Tom and I clambered down a rope ladder into a PT boat. Tom took the helm, I manned the radar, and a Greek sailor named Kyriakis stood by a MAG machine gun, mounted in the bows. Kyriakis was as handsome as a Greek god, with a tremendous physique. He was until quite recently an able seaman on a Greek freighter out of Piraeus but had jumped ship in Durban harbour after a fall-out with his bos'n over a tart in Point Road. Unfortunately he could speak only five words of English. The words he did know, which always made me laugh, were 'Greek e-sweet – English no e-sweet!' Which is how he got his nickname, Greeky Sweet. Even so, he understood a lot of the language, sweet or not, and we had no problem communicating with him.

Our recce went well. I noted several beaches which would do admirably for our landing, saw how they shelved and what the bottom consisted of. I was convinced nobody had seen us. If they had, we might expect a reception committee when we mounted the attack some weeks later. As quietly as we came, we pushed off back to *Ermans*. There she was, dark as sin, lying to her anchor, solid and dependable as ever. Before we turned in, Tom issued orders for the interdiction programme for that day. These entailed the use of four of the five PT boats. Off they went in the direction of Kigoma while the Mate shaped our course southwards for home, accompanied by the one remaining PT boat which we towed behind. I slept for six hours.

About noon we were twenty-five kilometres off the coast, more or less opposite Yungu. At this point the hinterland rises steeply from the lake to hills more than 2,000 feet high, close behind the town.

It then occurred to Tom that this might be a good chance to close with the shore and have a look at the fortifications of Yungu, which we ought to be able to see quite plainly from the lake. I liked the idea but thought it might be wiser if we did that from a PT boat which would not present quite such a good a target as *Ermans*. One never knew what long-range artillery the Cubans might have. So we turned *Ermans* through 90 degrees and headed her slowly for Yungu, intending to board the PT boat when we were about thirteen or fourteen kilometres off. *Ermans* would then remain in this vicinity until we returned, which should be in about an hour to two hours time.

As we lowered ourselves down the rope ladder into the PT boat, I realized with some surprise it was not the same boat that we had been in the night before. Indeed it wasn't. This one, could I believe my eyes, was actually armed with a 75 mm recoilless rifle, mounted slightly forward of amidships! Its long black barrel gleamed with evil intent, the breech covered, at the moment, with canvas. The gun had been mounted in such a way that it could fire abeam as well as forward. The base under its tripod mounting had been strengthened to absorb that downward thrust I talked about earlier. It looked a dangerous arrangement to me and I wasn't particularly chuffed with Tom for not telling me about the experimental nature of his armament. It was all to a good purpose, he explained. Air photos taken of Yungu by our Cuban air force in their T28s and B26s had revealed that there was a row of warehouses right down on the dockside. It was a safe bet that these contained hundreds of tons of arms and ammunition, ferried across from Kigoma. Tom's general plan had been that one of these days he would have a go at Yungu in this PT boat. Hence the armament. If he could get through the small gap in the sea wall which enclosed Yungu, he was certain he could do incalculable damage with this 75 mm cannon.

We pushed off from *Ermans*. Twenty minutes later, as we were closing with the land, a heavy curtain of mist came out of nowhere to drop on the surface of the lake, reducing visibility almost to zero. We slowed to three knots. From a navigation point of view the mist, which was not unusual on the lake at this time of year, presented no problem. Both *Ermans* and the PT boat were equipped with radar. On the contrary, it seemed to Tom, it presented us with a tremendous opportunity.

With some excitement he explained that the heavy mist was an amazing piece of luck. By navigating with radar we could actually approach Yungu and get right inside the harbour wall without detection. Then we could give the port and its installation one hell of a pasting with our 75 mm gun before the enemy knew we were there! He was probably right. A risk, of course, but not an unreasonable one. My blood began to race. I wasn't sure that it was entirely the sort of risk the commander of an infantry unit and his admiral ought to be taking at a time like this, but the odds were so very much in our favour that I decided to give it a go. The defenders would never expect an attack while the mist shrouded everything, and we would have the inestimable advantage of surprise. Great. The element of surprise, as I had always been taught, was the most important principle of war. Now we had it. Grasp it.

'What the hell,' said Tom; 'you only die once.'

'Laff when you say that,' I murmured.

Maximum visibility was now forty metres. We discussed a plan of action. We would approach very slowly, at about two knots, in the thick mist, and find the entrance to the port using our radar. Tom said this consisted of a twenty metre gap between two sea walls that jutted out in a semicircle from the bottom of a cliff. When we could see the gap clearly, we would dash in, stop, turn round and fire as many rounds as we could from the 75 mm cannon at point-blank range at the warehouses. With luck we would hit one or more containing ammunition. Chances were we wouldn't even be seen if the mist held. That done, we would scream out, rejoin *Ermans* and give each other the VC.

Sounded good to me.

Our radar was working perfectly. Already we were getting the shape of the port and the town behind it. Some of the larger warehouses were outlined clearly and getting clearer every minute.

'OK, Tom,' I said, 'subject to one thing.'

'What's that?'

'You're in command. I'm your number two for this operation. Greeky Sweet, if we make it, you become a sergeant as of now.'

I pointed to my arm and made three stripes across it.

Greeky Sweet got my drift, grinned and raised a thumb.

'OK, Mike. You take the helm, I'll take the gun. When I tell you I'm going to fire, you join me amidships and pass me the ammo. OK?'

'Aye, aye, sir.'

'Greeky Sweet – you stand in the bows with the MAG. Fire only when I give you an order. Got it?' Kyriakis nodded, cocked the weapon and checked the belt.

'Tom,' I asked, 'does the mist ever lift, suddenly?'

'Yes. Sometimes. But not very often.'

'What do we do if it does?'

'Turn round sharpish and go like buggery.'

I wondered how all this would sound in a court of enquiry, if it ever came to that, but decided to live the moment for what it was worth, even if it turned out to be our last.

Now I could see the walls of the port quite clearly on the radar screen. They were still about one kilometre away. I throttled right down, approaching gently at less than two knots, with hardly a ripple behind us and not a sound from the motor. We were as quiet as a ghost ship drifting noiselessly over the water. Tom began to run through the hand signals we might need, the ones for faster, slower, turn left, turn right, stop. The double signal would mean action! Full speed ahead, get into the port, stop, turn the boat right round – then Tom would blast off as many rounds as he could.

Tom loaded one of the big yellow-banded armour-piercing shells into the breech and locked it in position, holding the firing lanyard in one hand. Now we were less than 400 metres from the wall and closing fast. Three hundred. This is it, I said to myself, noticing a little quiver in the bowels. Mine own. Two hundred. The mist was holding and swirling round us, thickly. What luck! One hundred. Now I could hardly see the end of the boat. Fifty. Slower, slower.

Suddenly, out of nowhere came another boat! We heard it first and a few seconds later almost bumped into it. It was bearing down on us from the gap in the harbour wall. The crew had not seen us yet either, and it was just sheer coincidence and our bloody bad luck that they should be coming out precisely as we were going in. Tom didn't hesitate. He yelled at Kyriakis: 'Fire! Fire! Fire!' Greeky Sweet, firing from the hip, raked the enemy vessel with machine-gun fire from stem to stern, and then back again. The passengers and crew threw themselves into the water on all sides with yells of panic as their boat went completely out of control. A second or two later it exploded with an enormous bang and a hair-singeing whoosh of flame. Tom turned toward me rapidly, gave the double signal and pointed to the harbour gates.

'Full speed ahead!' he roared. 'Let's hit 'em!'

I gave her all she had. The boat leapt out of the water, bows up, as we jinked past the enemy boat right, then sharp left and then into the port through the gap in the wall. I knew exactly what I had to do. I slammed her into neutral and then gave her full astern, holding the helm over to starboard as hard as I could. She spun round and stopped. Greeky Sweet continued to fire long bursts in all directions, filling the air with the acrid smell of cordite.

'Up here, Mike, quick!'

I joined Tom. He was working the barrel-elevating wheel in a frenzy, lining the gun up on a warehouse which was emerging fast from the mist about eighty metres away. With a jerk of the lanyard he fired off the first shell. With an ear-splitting noise it hit the building plumb centre, went straight through it – and out the other side without explod-ing. 'Sod it!' he said. Tom reloaded with HE and took a slow, careful aim at another warehouse alongside. He jerked on the lanyard again. This time we hit the jackpot! With an almighty blast the whole dockside seemed to lift off the ground and explode in a huge ball of flame, bits and pieces of wood, stone and iron flying high into the air. The blast from the explosion bounced back on us, hit us abeam and rocked the boat dan-gerously. Bits of debris began to fall all round us as the blast echoed back again and again from the cliffside. Greeky Sweet, seeing a target now, kept up a steady machine-gun accompaniment, raking the wharf from end to end, enjoying the thrill of action, a wide grin all over his face. He was really living.

The mist began to lift. Maybe it was the heat from the burning buildings. Now we could see men running all over the dockside screaming orders to each other. One of them was wearing a chef's hat and white apron and had a big ladle in his hand. 'Three more for lunch, matey!' shouted Tom. At that moment a machine-gun opened up on us from a post sixty to seventy metres up the cliff side. Then another. They soon had our range, and bullets began to strike the water close by.

'Let's get the hell out of here!' shouted Tom.

I gave the engine maximum revs as we screamed through the opening in the harbour wall, snaking left and right, making for the open lake, Tom firing his FN at men on the harbour wall as we went. A full minute later we were out of range of the small-arms fire which was coming from a hundred different places all over the port and the hills behind us. We had poked a stick into a hornets' nest.

'Lot of bad boys there,' said Tom, wiping his forehead, as I eased up on the throttle. The bows dropped. We relaxed every pent-up muscle.'You all right, Kyriakis?'

Greeky Sweet was bent double, lying on the floor of the boat. Tom went forward and examined him gently. First he removed the belt of cartridges from his chest. They came away, full of blood. The Greek had been hit. Badly. Tom worked fast, lay him on his back, ripped open his clothing and slapped a first-aid dressing on his chest. He caught my eye and shook his head slowly. Tom took the gold chain and small crucifix off Greeky Sweet's neck, put them in his hand and closed his fist round them. Then he placed a life-vest under his neck and made him as comfortable as he could. He was as tender as a woman. Little though it was, there was nothing more he could do for the wounded man.

The mist seemed to be thicker out on the open water. Now we were making a steady twelve knots, due eastwards, looking for *Ermans*. I locked the helm in position and went forward to join Tom in the bows to see if there was anything I could do for Greeky Sweet. As I passed the gun amidships I looked down at the feet of the tripod and noticed a small spurt of water springing up from the bottom of the boat. That didn't seem right.

'Do these things ever leak, Tom?' I asked.

'Not so far,' he said. 'but there's always a first time. They're specially made of reinforced GRP in the States. State-of-the-art stuff. Why?'

'Just take a look at this.'

He came aft and inspected the leak.

'Seven bastards!' he shouted. 'We've cracked the flamin' hull!'

I stopped the boat. Now we were on an even keel we could examine the extent of the crack. It was just over one metre long, in places as much as ten millimetres wide, running fore and aft, exactly beneath the tripod. The water was seeping in steadily.

'Parallelogram of forces, Tom. There must have been one hell of a downward thrust from the blast.'

Tom said nothing but scanned the radar 180 degrees eastwards from north to south. And back again. He was looking for *Ermans*. He could find nothing on the screen. But she had to be there, somewhere.

'Radar's on the blink, Mike,' he said. 'Make 0-8-O. *Ermans* must be about ten or eleven kilometres off. Perhaps she'll show up when we're nearer. But hold her down to three knots.'

Now it was only a question of how long we could last. There was no point in bailing out. The water was coming in too fast. When the boat sank, we would have to swim for it. That's all there was to it. Tom threw me a life-vest.

'Use that if you want to die slowly,' he said. We laughed. It was an old joke in the ocean-going yachtsman's world.

'How long do you give it, Tom?' I asked.

'Who knows? Hour, two hours maybe, but the slower we go, the longer we'll last, that's for sure.'

We were travelling at less than two knots now and the water in the boat was already four inches deep. It still had quite a long way to go before it would stall the motor. Could we find *Ermans* before we sank? It was going to be a close-run thing. Meanwhile there was nothing much we could do but anticipate the worst. Tom went forward and had another look at Greeky Sweet. The Greek had lost all his colour and was gasping for air. Blackish blood was coming out of one side of his mouth. Tom supported him gently behind the neck and held his wrist for a few minutes. After a while the wounded man began to claw the air, tried to say something to Tom and sank back as though exhausted.

'I'm sorry, Mike,' said Tom, after a moment or two. 'I'm afraid Greeky Sweet's had it.'

Tom took off his yachting cap, looked down at his feet and

said a short prayer. 'Dear Lord. Please look after Greeky Sweet. He was a brave man. Please take him wherever brave men go.' I said 'Amen.' He covered Greeky Sweet's head with his jacket and came aft. We said nothing.

Ten minutes later we began to work out what we would do when the boat finally sank. Put on a life-jacket and swim very slowly for the shore was the only thing we could think of. And keep together. We might just make it. What happened if we did, we didn't discuss. That part of the shore was held by the enemy. The alternative was to try to stay where we were. Maybe *Ermans* would cruise around looking for us. We ruled that out as impractical. Pity they didn't have one of the PT boats with them, said Tom.

After a miserable hour we picked up a bleep on the radar in an easterly direction. That was most probably *Ermans*. Estimated range ten kilometres. Just over three hours away at this speed. It was no good: we would never make it, it was just too far. There were now eight inches of water in the hull.

The mist began to lift quickly. Now we could see the shore-line about four to five kilometres off. The sun was just beginning to dip behind the mountains. But it made a difference. Now our best bet was to turn round and make for the shore, come what may. The nearer we were to the shore when the boat sank, the better chance we had of survival. We turned in a big circle. The water level crept up and up.

A long hour later I thought I could hear the drone of an aeroplane. I cut the motor altogether. Then Tom heard it too. There in the far distance, away to the north of us, we could actually see something. It could be an aeroplane. It was. It was coming our way, it grew bigger as we watched it. Behind it were two others. They were flying in formation. The evening sun glinted on their wings. I knew them at once. They were ours! Our Cubans were doing their afternoon patrol. They always flew at 5,000 feet, just off the shoreline and out of range of small-arms fire.

Tom rummaged in a locker, got out the rockets and ripped open the canisters. There were only four. He readied them for firing. We waited, hearts beating fast. When the planes were nearing, he fired off two reds. They burst immediately above us. The planes went straight on as though they hadn't seen us. Tom fired off another and another as fast as he could. One of the planes waggled its wings! Then it broke formation, circled and dropped down low to see who or what we were. He screamed by us at zero feet. It was Mario Santachez, the leader of the Cuban pilots. I knew the number of his T28. We waved desperately and made signs to show him we were sinking. Mario banked steeply and came round again in a tight circle, waved his hand as if to say he'd got the message, and zoomed off to rejoin the other two planes.

'Don't know if he can do anything,' said Tom, 'but if there are any PT boats at base he could get one up here in two or three hours, I expect. But that's going to be too late for us. I give this tub another hour, maximum. Then we'll just have to tread water and hope for the best.'

It didn't sound too hopeful. I offered up a little prayer for help, as I always do when I have exhausted everything that I can do on my own. The God of soldiers and sailors I pray to has never failed me yet.

The boat sank at exactly 1705 hours. Sergeant Greeky Sweet's body went with it, never to be seen again. The lake here is nearly a kilometre deep. Tom and I trod water, wearing the yellow life-jackets the boat was equipped with. They held us up after a fashion but only just. What would happen when they became waterlogged I didn't care to think about. Our only hope was to swim for the shore, maybe six kilometres off, maybe more, so we struck out slowly and kept close together.

At exactly 1810 hours, just as dark was closing in on us, a black B26 and a single T28 circled the sky above us, dropping lower and lower with each circle. On his fourth circle the B26 must have caught sight of us, for he turned, came down almost to water level, opened the bomb-bay doors and dropped a yellow life-raft 200 metres away from us. It bounced several times and came to rest, upside down. The two planes circled until they could see we had made it, and then flew off home.

Getting the raft righted and getting into it was one hell of a job, but we made it. We lay on the bottom, exhausted and shivering with the cold. There was nothing we could do but wait until the following morning, when a PT boat would come out and find us. Which it did.

Six months passed. The rebellion was finally put down, even though Yungu itself was never captured, and for all I know

the rebels may still be there to this day. The place is impregnable, and I doubt if it could ever be taken short of a massive
air bombardment followed by an amphibious attack on a
grand scale.

It was the end of the road for me. I returned to Durban.
Tom wasn't there this time. He had already resumed his
single-handed voyage round the world in *Sundowner*. In due
course I had a card from him from St Helena, another from
Ascension Island and then one from Pernambuco on the
north-east coast of South America. He wintered in the Falk-
land Islands and took a job as a sheep-shearer.

When the time was right (that would be the following
spring, I guessed), he got under way again to round Cape
Horn, east to west. Half-way through the Strait of Magellan
the weather turned foul, or fouler than usual. The captain of
a Greek freighter reported seeing a small yacht hove-to in
mast-high seas, a tiny storm sail set. He signalled *Sundowner*.
Did Tom want any help? Tom put his head through the hatch
coaming and answered, no, he was all right.

That was the last that was ever seen or heard of *Sundowner*
or my brave friend Tom Harrison, that extraordinary Australian.

Some man.

3

A Cause Célèbre

Blessed is the commander who is assisted whole-heartedly by a loyal second in command. In Commandant Alistair Wicks I had just such a pearl. We operated in the time-honoured manner. My main duties would be operational, his would be administrative. But early on in the piece we had laughingly agreed that he and I would also make a general division of duties as between our main enemies – I would attend to the rebels, he would attend to the Belgians. The Belgians, at this time, saw us as interlopers in the Congo, the ex-colony they jealously regarded as their private preserve.

For this additional role Alistair was ideally suited. He was calm, polite, well bred, intellectual and astute. He was a European in every sense of the word, had travelled widely in his undergraduate days in eastern Europe and spoke excellent French and some German. This in itself was bordering on the unusual in a man who had been brought up at a time when Englishmen setting foot on the Continent were advised to speak slowly and clearly and to raise their voices as necessary in order to make themselves understood by those lesser breeds without the law, who, inconsiderately, could not speak the King's English. If I mention that he was educated at Harrow and Oxford you will understand that he had some depth of learning too. He had been trained as a lawyer at his university, and while he was not exactly 'full of wise saws and modern instances', he seemed never to have forgotten his case law, which he would dredge up whenever the occasion warranted it and from time to time when it didn't.

All of which contributed to my surprise one day when he stopped me outside the orderly room just as I was about to take CO's orders – the hearing of charges laid the previous day. Usually fairly minor stuff.

Alistair motioned me to one side. He was unusually agitated.

'There's a chap coming up this morning, sir, on a charge of desertion,' he explained, formally. 'He's our cook, if you can call that bastard a cook. A really bad sod. I have reason to believe he is going to come with some tricky technical defence. Please ignore it. I want you to make sure he gets the maximum the law, I mean you, can give him. If necessary, injustice must be done, but put him away for as long as you can. Like sixty days in the Memling. That should wipe the smile off his ugly mug.' He then added, *sotto voce* and out of range of the others, 'Hit him as hard as you can, Mike. He's a 'orrible bastard.'

'The Memling', by the way, was the name given to our punishment cell. It had no windows, and for this reason was also known as 'the room with no view'. It was named after the luxurious five-star hotel in Léopoldville. I laughed Alistair off. I thought it must be some sort of a joke. But he was serious. He was really worried that the accused might get away on some technicality. An interesting case of extra-sensory perception as it turned out. Alistair's prayer sparked off a remembrance of my days in India when I was a subaltern in 2 Reconnaissance Regiment. I recalled clearly reading an instruction from 2 Division Headquarters in Áhmednagar which cautioned commanding officers against those accused who were escaping their just punishment through clever defences and petty irregularities, such as, it was said, the charge's being improperly framed or not written in red ink, or whatever. I thought this might be something like that.

They might even have quoted the standard case which was doing the rounds at that time. That concerned an officer who had been arrested on the third floor of Shepheard's Hotel in Cairo in the act of chasing a young lady down a corridor at three o'clock in the morning, stark bollock naked. The officer, that is, not the lady. At his subsequent court martial his defence was impregnable. He claimed he was merely obeying Eighth Army standing orders, to wit: 'Officers will be appropriately dressed for the sport which they are pursuing.'

There were the usual minor cases to deal with before the great event of the day, and the only one that gave me any bother was a man named Pitout who was marched in and began to squirm around like a dancing dervish. No matter how many times the sergeant major would yell at him to stand still, he continued to jump from foot to foot. A few seconds later all became clear when his trousers broke into spontaneous flame. He had stuffed a lighted cigarette into his trouser pocket seconds before being wheeled in.

Although we operated under no military legal code whatsoever, other than that which I could remember vaguely from my previous study of the *Manual of Military Law*, nobody ever complained. It wouldn't have done them much good if they had. Alistair and I and the RSM pooled our small knowledge of that heavy tome as and when required. In the main it consisted, as we all remembered, of Section 40, which was so widely framed as to allow for any possible crime which our men were likely to commit, and that could be described under the general heading of 'conduct to the prejudice of good order and military discipline'. But in the course of the next two years my bold warriors were able to show me how much I had underestimated their potential for getting into trouble, and Section 40 proved less than adequate.

In addition to our general knowledge of the law relating to soldiery we each made a more arcane contribution. Mine was the definition of mutiny, which I remembered from the manual. Private Atkins (obviously a Victorian soldier), divesting himself of his waist belt and throwing it down at his feet, proclaims, 'I will soldier no more. You may do what you like.' Stirring words for a private in the days when the lash and being tied to a gun wheel were not uncommon punishments for fairly minor infringements of the disciplinary code. As a result I had always admired the animus which motivated Private Atkins, but as mutiny was hardly to be expected among voluntary mercenary soldiers who could resign whenever they wished, and as waist belts were an unknown quantity, my contribution added little to our store of knowledge. In passing, may I say I was wrong again. Mutiny occurred twice during my service in the Congo.

Alistair did better, with a specious and rather surprising understanding of the laws relating to sodomy, with, need I say, supporting case law. Neither of us could see any immediate application for that one either. We hoped not, anyway. But it was a verbatim quotation from the aforesaid *Manual of Military Law* which the RSM had off by heart which restored the average and vindicated our metaphorical wearing of wigs and gowns. It was Section 99, he seemed to think, which had to do with the infamy of wearing long hair and being unshaven. I shuddered in mock despair at the very thought. The RSM laid it on the line: 'The 'air of the 'ed will be kep' short. The chin and underlip will be shaven. Whiskers if worn will be of a moderate length!'

Armed with this legal expertise we faced all malefactors, malapert knaves and other rogues, with whom 5 Commando in its early days was heavily endowed, with complete confidence. The first case concerned a man who had the temerity to defy unit orders by trying to grow a beard. I had made it clear that there would be no bearded wonders with me. That was the sole prerogative of *les affreux*. Not that I have anything against beards as such, but I am convinced that beards on active service conditions in Africa, with its heat and dust, are unhealthy and difficult to keep clean. I may be old-fashioned but I also think they look unsoldierly. The last thing I wanted was for my men to look like a bunch of Zouaves, good lads though I am sure they are. Furthermore beards rob a man of that feeling of super-cleanliness which comes from a good daily shave, the greatest morale-builder known to military science – apart of course from a co-operative and nubile girlfriend. And in this connection let us not forget the old Polish army saying, 'Women are the relaxation of warriors.'

The charge against the bearded one was supported by a reading of the statute against beards as stated in the standing orders. The evidence was damning and self-evident. There was no defence. Apart from being told to get the foliage off at once, the dastardly criminal escaped punishment. 'Admonished,' I wrote on the crime sheet, a word whose meaning, in this context, I have never really understood.

Then it was time for the accused cook, a gentleman born within the sound of Bow Bells by the sound of him, to come before the majesty of the law. He was marched in in the approved fashion with his cap off. Left right, left right, left right, left, halt. Left turn. The charge was read out all in one breath in that extraordinary way regimental sergeant majors delight in.

'How do you plead?'

'Not guilty, sir.'

'You are employed in the cookhouse?'

'Yes, sir. I am the head cook. I have five other cooks under me.'

'How are you managing?'

'I was dóing all right until just recent.'

'What happened?'

'The blokes started to moan. It's not my fault if the rations ain't up to much, is it? Can't work bleedin' miracles, can I?'

'That'll do!' hissed the sergeant major, prodding the accused in the small of his back. 'Watch your language in front of the CO.'

All armies perpetuate the myth that commanding officers are as pure as the driven snow when taking orders and that their innocent ears must be protected from foul language.

'So what happened then?'

'Well, I got browned off, didn't I? I decided to scarper. I got me feelin's too, you know, sir.' The touch of pathos went straight to my stony heart.

At this stage the RSM decided to interpret. For the purpose of CO's orders the commanding officer is regarded as an imbecile to whom the simplest matters have to be explained in distressing detail.

'Scarper, sir. Rhyming slang. Scapa Flow, go. He went, sir.'

'Thank you, Sergeant Major. Proceed.'

'Well, I walked to Kaminaville, didn't I? And then I took a train to E'ville. Just to get a bit of a break like.'

Two days later he was picked up by the military police in Élisabethville, drunk as a skunk. An open-and-shut case as they say in legal circles, if Hollywood, my tutor in these things, is to be believed.

Now it was his turn to defend himself.

'Anything you wish to say?'

I was fingering the black cap under my desk.

'All as I can say, sir,' he began, in measured tones, well rehearsed, I have no doubt, before his barrack-room-lawyer buddies -'all as I can say is that I did not desert. Definitely not, sir. I may have absented myself from barracks without permission' – he liked the sound of that, so he repeated it, – 'I may have absented myself from barracks without permission, but as to desertion, no, sir. Definitely not.'

He seemed to understand the gravity attached to a charge of desertion. Somebody must have warned him about the difference between that and absenting oneself without leave, a lesser matter. He paused for dramatic effect, then dropped his blockbuster.

'In any case I was only obeying orders.'

'Obeying orders?'

The court's collective imagination boggled. This new twist in the legal argument galvanized all present.

'How so?'

'May I call Commandant Wicks as a witness, sir?'

If the case was being heard on appeal in the House of Lords, it could hardly have caused a greater stir. Alistair came in like a greyhound let off the leash. Hardly surprising, seeing that he had had his ear glued to the door.

The accused cross-examined the Commandant.

'Commandant Wicks, sir, did you or did you not say to me in the cookhouse on the morning of the eleventh instant: 'Dogsbody, as a cook you are a bleeding disaster; as a soldier you are a screaming abortion; bugger off and don't you ever let me see your ugly face again!' '

'Quite likely. Why?'

'Well, that's just what I done, sir. Buggered off. Obeyed them orders, just like you told me to do.'

Case dismissed.

What else could I do? Got me feelin's too, ain't I? And a sense of humour.

Kind hands helped the apoplectic commandant to his quarters.

4
The Big Game Hunter

Some years ago I was driving my five-ton truck across the south-eastern border of Angola into north-western Bechuanaland (now called Botswana). My destination was Maun, the tiny mud-hut capital of Ngamiland. The journey usually took me two days from the border. The track passed through some very heavy sand belts, hemmed in by youthful mopani trees, flat-topped acacias and an occasional borassus palm. It was pretty rough going, but no problem if you took it slowly and had a vehicle which spoored with the track, as mine did. My route lay southwards past Shakawe, a small but important village on the headwaters of the Okavango delta, and then on another 160 kilometres or so past a place called Tsau, a trading post on the edge of the Kalahari desert.

I churned along slowly in bottom gear, hoping to make Maun by nightfall. I suppose I was making about twenty-five kilometres in the hour, not bad for this part of the world. Some distance beyond Tsau three young white men emerged from the bush and waved me down, which was very unusual. In the Bechuanaland Protectorate in those days (and I imagine it is no different today) it was unheard-of not to stop to give assistance to anybody that might need it. So I stopped. The three had been hunting and wanted a lift to a village called Sehitwa, about sixty kilometres further on. But before they loaded their 'bag' onto the back of my truck I asked if I might see what it comprised. This was a very natural precaution. I had to satisfy myself there was no Royal Game in it. A young kudu doe, two impala and a steenbuck were the sum total. Nothing abnormal there. They hoisted the animals onto the truck, clambered on top and off we went.

Let me explain at this point that the laws which prohibited

the shooting of Royal Game in Ngamiland were draconian, and very rightly so. They provided for a massive fine and the confiscation of a hunter's weapons and vehicles on conviction. This and the opprobrium which would attach to such a sentence were sufficient to write *finis* to a hunter's career. Royal Game included the delectable eland, hippo, rhino and certain of the cats but not, of course, lion, which at this time was classed as vermin and could be hunted freely.

It was well known in Ngamiland that a family of cheetahs had been seen in the park-like area we were now crossing, and they had, of course, been declared Royal Game and their presence widely advertised. Not only were cheetahs an extremely rare species in this part of the world but their numbers in general were thought to be declining almost everywhere on the African continent, so that conservationists, and hunters in particular, were taking a great interest in their preservation. So you may imagine my delight and astonishment when barely another ten miles further on the leader of the cheetah pack broke through the bush and leapt across the track not twenty metres in front of my truck, to be followed one at a time by the rest of his family at intervals of a few seconds. I stopped, spellbound, as I watched these graceful creatures lope through the waist high grass until they disappeared from my view.

I turned in my seat to see if the chaps on the back of the truck had spotted the cheetahs – only to freeze with horror when I saw two of them raise their rifles and fire in the direction of the disappearing animals. A volley crashed out. I screamed out to them to stop firing, jumped from the cab and raced through the bush on foot to see if any of the cheetahs had been hit. There was no trace of them.

When I got back to the truck I demanded an explanation from the hitch-hikers. Far from being apologetic or making any excuses for their action, they brazened it out until I became angry. The upshot of the affair was that I told them to get off my truck and walk the rest of the way to Sehitwa, thirty-five kilometres further on, no great hardship and a small matter compared with the penalty I would have incurred if it became known that my vehicle had been used for the shooting of Royal Game, and this Royal Game in particular.

One of the three young men was an exceptionally handsome Cypriot whom I had met before and knew as the spoilt son of a wealthy trader in this area. His name was Demetriou. He had had a few brushes with the law already, mostly minor offences to do with hunting, and had always relied on his rich father to bail him out whenever the going got too rough. I often wondered how things would turn out for him.

Strangely enough it was at Kamina Base in Katanga, a year later, that our paths crossed again. My unit, 5 Commando, was in formation. Recruiting for the unit was in full flow, so that planes from Johannesburg and Salisbury would bring in more men for the unit almost daily. An hour after their arrival they were paraded for my inspection. On this occasion I noticed a familiar face among the new intake. It was Demetriou. Within days his fame as a big game hunter went out before him. Most evenings would find him in the canteen seeking the bubble reputation, even in the lion's mouth! His new-found mates were vastly impressed with the stories he told them of dropping rogue elephants at fifteen metres, lions as they were making their final leap, and buffalo that kept on charging long after they were dead but didn't know it. But it was his self-proclaimed ability with the heavy-bore stuff, the animals he had killed, the trophies he had won, how his name appeared in Roland Ward etc, which got among them. They were vastly impressed. Most of them had never seen a wild animal outside a zoo, never mind hunted one.

So it only took a day or two before a match in marksmanship was arranged between him and some of the old hands on the rifle range. A book was made. Demetriou was backed down to even money by his fans and those who believed his stories, which were pretty plausible. His stock was high.

The meeting was held on a Saturday afternoon. There were two contests, application and grouping, both at 300 metres. In the former he failed miserably, in the latter he was a near disaster. The old sweats made mincemeat of him. Now the knives were out for the handsome young Cypriot, but he rode it out calmly. As he said, you can't compare an FN rifle with a 30-0-6, the sort of precision job he was used to. Not that anyone agreed with him.

Even that didn't really cut him down to size. Surprisingly enough it was only a small thing that did it. The way a mercenary soldier dresses and adorns himself with arma-ment of one sort or another is very often an indication of his prowess in the field and certainly gives one an insight into his character. My experience has been, in general, that those soldiers who delight in festooning themselves with knives, grenades, belts of ammo etc, are less likely to turn out to be good infantrymen than the unostentatious types who are happy to carry standard equipment. A sort of inverse proportion rules. Demetriou had everything that money could provide on his person in the way of weaponry – including two bandoliers criss-crossed on his chest South American bandit style, several grenades hooked into his belt, and an ivory-handled revolver on each hip. An impressive sight you might say. And he had the presence and charisma to go with it.

What topped it off, and caused his eventual downfall, was the bone-handled hunting knife which stuck out of the top of his calf-length leather boots, which were, of course, need I say it, lined with pure white sheepskin.

As soon as the men saw him in this fancy rig they called him 'Puss in Boots'. The name stuck. He couldn't take it. He resigned shortly afterwards.

5

Mon Général

It was Léopoldville, July 1964. The captains and the kings had departed. After four inglorious years the United Nations peace-keeping forces in the Democratic Republic of the Congo had folded their tents and gone home, taking their tarnished record with them. The very next day, literally, Mr Moise Tshombe, who had been languishing in exile in Madrid, was invited back to the Congo to become its new prime minister. Unbelievable, but true. All the rancour of the last few years had been swept aside, the charge that he had been responsible for the murder of Patrice Lumumba pushed under the carpet. The bitterness engendered by the rise and fall of the Independent State of Katanga became a thing of the past – *ça c'est le Congo!*

This extraordinary event, the return of the prodigal son as it were, took the international press completely by surprise. It hurried to Léopoldville to see what was cooking. In no time at all the city was bursting at its seams with people looking for accommodation. Every hotel was booked solid and many journalists were obliged to sleep in their hired cars.

One of the first things Mr Tshombe did on his return from exile was to send for Alistair Wicks and myself. It was possible he might need a force of mercenary soldiers to support the National Army, he said, if there proved to be no other way of stopping the advance of the rebels who were now reported to be only one hundred kilometres from the capital and advancing. In less than three months the rebellion had threatened to engulf the whole of the Congo, and there was no knowing where it might end. It was obvious that some urgent and effective military action was needed if the rebels were to be stopped at the gates of the capital. The Congolese National

Army were plainly ineffective and in many cases had fled in the face of the enemy, terrified by the threat of witchcraft, a potent force in Africa to this day. But first Mr Tshombe was going to try a policy of reconciliation, to which end he set forth at once on a swift tour of the country, holding out the olive branch. It was doomed to failure.

Meanwhile we were installed in some comfort at the Memling Hotel, a five-star establishment in Léopoldville, as the guests of the new prime minister, and told to await his call. One day he might send for us to say he needed that force of mercenary soldiers to assist the Congolese National Army fight the rebels. We simply had to be patient and wait. In the meantime our greatest enemy was boredom. There was nothing to do but study the local papers and listen to the BBC announce the inexorable advance of the rag-tag army of rebels on Léopoldville.

When I was not doing that, I was usually listening spellbound to a new American friend I had met by chance in the foyer of the hotel. He was larger than life and twice as natural, and if you searched the earth three times over you would not find his like. His name was Hubert Fauntleroy Julian, Colonel Julian. He wore a gold rimmed monocle in his left eye and spoke with a resounding musical voice which could reach all corners of the largest room. He stood six foot six in his socks and was about two foot broad all the way up to his bull neck. He was a magnificent specimen of humanity and although he was actually well into his seventies he acted and looked as if he was in his middle fifties. But he worked at it. He never drank alcoholic liquors, was highly selective in what he ate, to the point of distraction, never ate more than one big meal a day and walked everywhere whenever he could. He began his day with a litre of clear still water which had to be bottled and was, preferably, Evian. His wardrobe was carefully chosen and his linen spotless. In his cravat he sported a diamond pin in the shape of a horseshoe. Come evening time, when I would accompany him around town, he always wore a three-quarter-length opera cloak fastened at the neck by a heavy silver chain. The cloak was lined with red silk. He never wore a hat but always sported a silver-knobbed ebony cane. The total effect was highly theatrical, of course, but he could carry it off with distinction. When we parted each evening in the lobby, he would wrap me in his cloak and kiss me on both

cheeks! He did it as though he was conferring on me the
Congressional Medal of Honour.

I love a real character, particularly one who is unconven-
tional and able to defy the ridiculous rules of civilization
which hem us in. Colonel Julian was the genuine article. His
French was something else again and had been learned in
Martinique, he claimed. Even allowing for his irregular syn-
tax and singular pronunciation he had no problems with
communication. It was just another facet of his sparkling
personality.

But all things considered it was his background that set you
back on your heels. He'd come a long way in his seventy-odd
years, overcoming unfair difficulties which the majority of us
don't even know exist. He had a knack of attracting the
limelight. He was an aviator and the first man ever to parachute down onto Brooklyn, and that was way back in 1925.
He held the dubious distinction of having been responsible
for the single-handed destruction of half the Abyssinian air
force in the early thirties. They had two planes at the time and
he crashed one of them! He established records for solo flights
all over the USA in the early days of flying.

He entertained me by the hour with his marvellous Yankee
drawl and fund of true stories. The one I liked best occurred
back in the thirties. He was flying south from New York on a
mission to Mexico when he was obliged to make a forced
landing from lack of fuel on a lonely airfield somewhere in
Kentucky. He taxied right up to the control tower, jumped
down from the cockpit and went up the steps. As he removed
his flying helmet and scarf, the controller's face registered
dismay. The colonel asked him to ring up for a taxi cab to take
him into town. The ensuing telephone conversation ran this-
a-way:

'Hi ya, Jake. Kin you send a cab to the airfield right away?
I got me a pilot wants to get into town while we fuel up his
plane.'

'Sure thing, Bud. Who's it for?'

'Some guy named Julian. Better tell you now, Jake, he's a
coloured gennelman. That OK with you?'

'You mean this here pilot's a nigger?'

'Shure 'nuff. But, Bud, listen man, this ain't no ordinary
nigger!'

Hubert would go into paroxysms of laughter every time he

told me that story. I hope the story gives no offence, it certainly isn't intended to do so, but I suppose that's what the southern states of America were like in the thirties. In any case I can confidently say nothing like that ever hurt Colonel Julian. He was too big a man in every way.

Well, what was he doing here now? He'd come to see Tshombe, whom he regarded as a personal friend. Knew him in his Katanga days, he said. Like the rest of the world, it seemed, now that the great man was back in power, he was here to collect.

He hung around for a week or two but never did get to see the prime minister who was, of course, far too busy. Tshombe's waiting room was full to overflowing day after day from early morning until late into the night. That waiting-room became notorious. When the prime minister was being entertained some months later in London by some members of the Conservative Party, he was introduced to an admirer, a senior member of the House of Lords.

'You must visit me when you come to Léopoldville,' said Mr Tshombe.

'But I was there for one week about a month ago,' said his Lordship.

'And did you enjoy your time in our beautiful city?'

'No, can't say I did. I spent all of it in your waiting-room!'

One evening about a fortnight later I was loitering in the foyer watching the Congolese hotel receptionists turn away would-be guests by the drove. One such was thumping the counter with a lot of bluster and very little finesse. Even though his French was excellent, he was getting nowhere.

'*Complet! Complet! Complet!*' one of the little clerks repeated impassively as he turned his back on him.

Frustrated beyond endurance the newcomer walked over to me and asked me, in English, if I had any influence in this benighted hole. I hadn't, of course. He introduced himself. He was an officer in the South African Defence Force, major-general actually, he said in an off-hand manner, lately military attaché at his country's embassy in Paris. Just arrived by UTA from Johannesburg, he explained. Didn't expect the place to be so damned crowded. We chatted amiably for a few minutes.

He seemed a pleasant enough chap and as I had a spare bed in my room I felt it would be churlish not to offer it to him.

He thanked me briefly and accepted the offer as though it was, after all, his due, and just what he would have expected of me.

In the days that followed I came to know him as what I imagined to be the archetype senior South African army officer, unimaginative and painfully correct. Regrettably he was also as dull as ditchwater and entirely without a sense of humour. Worse than that, I soon discovered he was bigoted and didactic in all things concerning the perilous military situation in the Congo.

What his brief was, or why he was there at all, I was too polite to ask, but I guessed, probably correctly, that he had been sent by the South African Defence Force to see what assistance General Mobutu might need in his present difficulties. I gathered this from his appearance on several successive days outside the C-in-C's inner sanctum at Quartier Général, patiently waiting for an interview. I could have told him that much more important people than he, a mere major-general, had given up all hope of ever seeing Mobutu and had returned from whence they came, despairing of the new regime.

Even so General R and I became, by virtue of our forced companionship, quite friendly. He called me by my Christian name, but on my side I was never able to discover what his first name might be. I wouldn't have used it in any case. I was a patient listener to his interminable assessments of the military situation in the Congo and what Mobutu ought and ought not to do next. One evening he announced that he had at long last secured an audience with the Commander-in-Chief. I listened with mounting disbelief as he told me how he intended to conduct himself at the interview.

'I am going to tell him in the simplest possible terms what's wrong with his strategy and show him what he ought to do. He's making a balls of it, Mike. Distributing his forces in penny packets all over the country … no overall plan of campaign, just reacting to rebel attacks when and where they occur … insufficient use of air … failure to use his information services … ' On and on he went.

I was hypnotized by the crassness of his intended approach and sat dumb. He must have taken this for tacit agreement with his plan of campaign. He looked to me now for some comment, an unusual occurrence. In fact I was more than grateful for the chance to say something which could be helpful. My experience in Africa in this sort of thing was probably greater than his, although I would never have said so. Emboldened by the closeness of our acquaintanceship over the last few days, I took it upon myself to offer him some advice, acutely conscious of the fact that he was a major-general and I was a nothing.

'*Mon général,*' I began (he liked that mode of address), 'please don't do it. At least, please don't do it that way. If I may say so, you don't know these chaps like I know them. They are understandably sensitive to the least criticism of their ability as military leaders. In any case, sir, it's their show, not ours. They are entitled to run it in any way they think best. I promise you that if you go in there tomorrow and start telling Mobutu how to run his army, he will have you escorted onto the next plane south before you can say Paul Kruger. Don't do it, sir, I beg of you. You can say the same thing in a hundred different ways without giving offence.'

I developed the theme and thought I was being pretty persuasive. The general snorted and took another shot from my Ballantynes.

'Rubbish, old man. These chaps have got to be told. Can't blame them, not their fault. It's all a question of experience, isn't it? Most of them have never had any formal training above sergeant. Not a single Congolese in the Force Publique above the rank of sergeant major at the time of independence they tell me. Extraordinary state of affairs. Don't know what the Belgians thought they were up to!'

There was no moving him. I closed my eyes in contemplation of the interview. What came to mind was the picture of an unstoppable bulldozer grinding along in bottom gear as it approached the edge of a precipice; the driver was a man with a red band round his hat.

I had to leave Léopoldville for a day or two, so I said goodbye to *mon général*. He thanked me for the bed, said he would be off home in a few days and hoped that when this show was over I would contact him in Pretoria as he would like to offer me a job on his staff. I thanked him in turn and said I looked forward to meeting him again one day.

I heard in due course from the aide-de-camp to the C-in-C that my general had indeed given his advice in the manner he had planned and that Mobutu's reaction to it was entirely as I had foretold. My general had been invited firmly to board the next plane to South Africa. In fact they thought so much of him they even supplied an armed escort to Ndjili to see he didn't miss it.

A small and not particularly earth-shaking snippet about those days but it had a sequel which may not bore you.

Two years later, when my service in the Congo was over, I had occasion to visit Pretoria. I thought it might be nice to see *mon général* again. I called at Defence Headquarters in Potgieter Street and sent in a request to see him. He was there, but not available. I left my name and the name of my hotel, with a request that he should ring me. Nothing heard. I tried again to contact him in the next two days, without success. I left a message, this time with my home address. I followed this with a letter. There was no reply.

But a month or so later I received a telephone call from Commandant Vic Jearey, who had been senior staff officer to the general when he was in Durban two years previously. Vic and I had become friends in the interval. Jearey was a superb military man, knowledgeable, patient and articulate. Now his voice was overladen with an awful embarrassment.

'I have a message for you from Pretoria, Mike,' he began, with some hesitation, 'but it's so shabby I hate to give it to you. But as it is my duty, I suppose I must. It is from General R. He says that the next time you are in Pretoria please pop round to the mess *after dinner* for a cup of coffee. If you can let him know in advance, he will make sure there are one or two officers there to listen to some of your Congo experiences.'

I laughed. *Mon général* had not changed much with the years.

6

A Sign from Heaven

One of my 5 Commando rules for battle read 'Pray God daily.' Many of my men obeyed that instruction punctiliously; some even read their Bibles day by day like the famous General Gordon of Khartoum. But I always noticed a subtle change of mood among the men when combat was imminent. It was a time when many of them sought refuge in prayer. What their motivation may have been I could not say. Perhaps it was the 'dread of something after death, the undiscovered country, from whose bourn no traveller returns'. The subject of their prayers, I would lay even money, was themselves, their welfare, their self-preservation, that they should be spared. Natural enough.

From personal observation I am convinced that this belief in the Almighty, and in the power of prayer, is common to all those who come face to face with the awesome forces of nature or who are subject to dangers which are beyond their control. Soldiers on the eve of battle seek the hand of God. That I do know. It is something which comes naturally, even to the most hardened of old sweats. Sometimes their faith is weak and they look for some tangible sign, some signal which will tell them their prayer will be answered. Sometimes they get it.

Orders had been received for 5 Commando to advance against the enemy in the Oriental province of the Congo at once. Intelligence had confirmed that the enemy had been preparing fortified positions for some months past. On the face of things it looked as though the unit might be in for a rough time. If we were to judge by the law of averages, our casualty rate would be high. The supposition was that one in four men would be killed or seriously wounded.

Action, actual contact with the enemy, was to begin the next day, a Monday. The thought gave us pause. This was the moment of truth, the moment when every man might have to face his Maker. Holy Joe, the unit's honorary lay pastor, sensing the mood of the men, asked permission to conduct a drumhead service on the Sunday morning before we moved up to our battle positions.

Two hundred or so men gathered round him in a half-circle on a high piece of ground, hats off, eyes lowered, and intoned the old familiar prayers and sang the old familiar hymns. Close by a radio truck had established a signal station. 5 Commando signallers were busy making contact with Army Headquarters in Léopoldville, 2,000 kilometres away – no problem on a Collins single-side-band transmitter-receiver.

'O Lord, hear our prayer,' sang out Holy Joe.

'Hearing you loud and clear!' came a robust voice from the radio truck, confirming God's omnipresence.

The sign the old sweats looked for had been vouchsafed.

7

A Time To Go

The red tail plane of a DC7b glinted in the clear blue sky above Albertville. The aircraft circled widely over Lake Tanganyika and then dropped low over our barracks as though to warn us it was about to land. Jack Malloch was bringing us a fresh contingent of men. Excitement rippled through the unit. We had been waiting eagerly for this intake. These new men would complete our establishment for the third contract, which was due to begin in a day or two.

Each contract was for a period of six months. Doesn't sound long, but in the Congo, and under our service conditions, it was an age. Very few men completed more than one contract, apart of course from the hard-bitten professionals, the real mercenary soldiers, to whom this was a way of life that could go on for ever as far as they were concerned. They came again and again, just using the period between contracts as a time to go on an almighty thrash until their money was spent. The men were all volunteers and had the right to resign at any time during the contract if they so wished. Not many men took advantage of this clause, possibly because there were heavy monetary penalties attached to the option. There was also the question of loss of face, which was of some importance to quite a number of them.

Soon after their arrival I made it my business to interview each man individually, to make absolutely certain he understood what he was volunteering for and what would be expected of him. I had found this routine to be essential. Large numbers of recruits arrived with romantic notions of mercenary soldiering, founded on half-understood stories of the French Foreign Legion. 'The Beau Geste' syndrome Alistair and I called it. As a result of these interviews I usually found it necessary to reject a large number of the newcomers, many of whom were chancers, booze artists, drug-addicts, bums who had bribed the recruiting officers, every possible type you can imagine.

This time it was worse than ever. The recruiting officers in Salisbury and Johannesburg were obviously having to scrape the bottom of the barrel. More than 2,000 men had been through my hands in the last twelve months in this way, so I was not altogether surprised at the drop in standards. Now that the newspapers were carrying stories of the number of mercenary soldiers killed or seriously wounded, the flow of volunteers was beginning to dry up, so that when I came to interview this particular draft I found over fifty per cent of them unsuitable. They would have to go back on the plane that brought them. The quality of the men they were sending me now was too low. I could never train them in the time available.

A bad soldier is not only a liability to his unit: he is also, in action, a positive menace and a danger to his comrades. It usually comes as a surprise to civilians to learn that a high percentage of casualties on active service, more in action, are caused by accidents attributable to a low standard of training. Sometimes these casualties exceed those inflicted by the enemy. Take the simplest of all instructions relating to the handling of weapons: finger on the trigger guard at all times, never on the trigger, until you are actually going to fire. If soldiers obeyed that basic rule, the numbers killed by accident, usually in barracks, would be considerably less. But hardly a month goes by but one reads of a firearm's being accidentally discharged, sometimes with fatal results.

As far as officer potential was concerned, in this intake there was the usual dearth. That didn't surprise me. A man who would make a good junior officer would also make a good junior executive in the commercial world. Such a man would be unlikely to disturb his career for the adventure of mercenary soldiering, even if he saw it in that light. Officers in mercenary units tend to be promoted from the ranks and are seldom given officer rank at the time of recruitment. Mercenary army officers are a breed totally different from those who graduate from military academies such as Sandhurst or West Point. Mercenary officers are less concerned with the administration of troops than regulars. Tradition and protocol are of zero importance. They are more concerned with the immediacy of action, the basic reason for their employment. As a result those soldiers who have proved themselves in combat are usually the ones who are promoted to officer rank, sometimes very speedily and often in the field. Promotion has nothing to do with a man's background, his education, who his parents were, whether or not his forebears served in the regiment, what sort of an accent he speaks with, the colour of his skin etc. It has everything to do with his ability to lead men in the field. Perhaps it ought to be like this in the great big world of commerce outside, the real world as they say, but it isn't. Sometimes the opportunity of rapid promotion is given to a man as the result of attrition. On a previous contract one of my sergeants ended up as a captain in command of his unit largely because his five previous commanders were killed or wounded before him in quick succession.

Knowing all this, I was considerably surprised when Frank Amberleigh was shown in for the usual interview. He was about thirty-three, clean cut, fit and confident and until quite recently an officer in the Bechuanaland Protectorate administration. I remembered him well from the days when I conducted safaris in the Okavango delta. He had been a district officer at Kasane, where the Chobe and the Zambesi rivers meet. Lovely spot with fantastic tiger fish giving battle all the way to the transom. Over the years we had become good friends. I welcomed him warmly. It was good to see an old familiar face once again and to talk over old times. We chatted inconsequentially before getting down to business.

'Tell me, Frank, what brings you here?' It was my stock question.

'I need the money, sir.' It was the stock answer.

'Perhaps I ought to tell you, Frank, that money of itself is not really a sufficient reason for soldiering in the Congo in the way we do. The risks are out of all proportion to the money you may earn. Perhaps you don't know it but we lose one out of four men in actual combat from death, wounds and disease. A wound in this heat, no matter how slight, stands a good chance of going gangrenous. You know what that means?'

I chopped at an arm. He nodded.

'This is not anything like regular army soldiering. We don't have any administrative back-up to speak of. We carry our house around with us wherever we go, like snails. Our medical facilities, for instance, are rudimentary. Sufficient for normal conditions but insufficient for a prolonged campaign. When a man gets seriously wounded, everything depends on the speed with which we can evacuate him to a base hospital, if we are to save his life. Sometimes we are lucky and we have a helicopter at our disposal; sometimes we're not.'

I was painting the picture a little blacker than it deserved, but he was an intelligent man and I wanted him to appreciate some of the problems of mercenary soldiering and why it was necessary to bring a certain attitude to the life.

'No, Frank, there's got to be something more to it than just the money. You've got to want to do it for some other reason – like a love of soldiering for itself, for instance, or the joy and fulfilment that you may get from the command of men. Or it may be that you are furthering your political motivation in some way. But there's got to be some compelling reason that will make it seem worthwhile for you. Money is important, of course, but for an intelligent man it's not enough. There are easier ways of making a living than that. You get my drift?'

He began to consider these unpalatable facts, facts which he obviously hadn't considered before or perhaps even found it necessary to consider. He had heard that mercenary soldiers were paid very well and he needed money. That was all there was to it. But the facts had given him pause.

I switched the subject.

'And how are Marie and the kids?' I remembered his wife as a beautiful woman with three lovely young daughters, all images of him.

'Fine,' he said, 'just fine.' He grinned. 'I see there's an indemnity clause in the contract which says a man's widow gets $20,000 US if he gets killed, and each child gets a further $2,000. They'll be rich if anything happens to me!'

We laughed, but I thought I'd better give him time to think the whole thing over now that he knew more about the conditions of service. I imagined they were vastly different from those he had expected. I suggested he take a day to think it over. Jack Malloch's plane was due to go back to Salisbury thirty-six hours later, so Frank had plenty of time to change his mind. But before he went I said that if he decided to stay

I would give him a commando of his own and the rank of captain. With hindsight I see this was an error. But it was not intended as some sort of bait, I just wanted him to know how he stood.

The next day he confirmed his decision to stay. I introduced him to his new command and sent him off to a forward position which was in contact with the enemy. Rebel troops had landed on the west coast of Lake Tanganyika from bases in Tanganyika just south of Kigoma, and had established themselves near a town called Kahimba, about fifty kilometres north of Albertville. This unusual situation provided a unique opportunity for advanced training. Nothing sharpens up a man's reflexes like the possibility of bumping into the enemy at any time.

Reports began to reach me of his unit's steady progress in training and of the esteem in which Frank was held by his men. He was plainly the traditional officer type, a type not often found in mercenary units, and as such had little difficulty in maintaining discipline. Why it should be easier for an officer to lead and command just because he comes from a higher social level than his men is an interesting problem, but not one I am going to burden you with now. Let us just accept, for the moment, that this happens to be so.

Meanwhile the remainder of the unit began to take shape and I busied myself with the plan for the next operation, which was scheduled to start in six weeks. Armoured vehicles, arms and ammunition, communications equipment, all the paraphernalia of modern warfare began to arrive in a steady stream via the efficient Belgian staff in Albertville. Excitement in the unit started to mount. Men took their training seriously, drank less and wrote more letters home. The unit developed a cohesive spirit. There is nothing to lift the morale of soldiers like the certainty of going into action.

Five weeks later, almost on the eve of our departure for our assembly point, I had an unexpected visit from Frank. He was obviously greatly distressed. He had come to hand in his resignation! I couldn't believe it. But why? Some tragedy at home perhaps? But no. Nothing like that. He had thought it all over for the hundredth time, he said, and had finally come to the conclusion that he was being grossly unfair to his wife and kids. What would happen to them if he should be killed or seriously wounded, blinded perhaps? He had been turning this thought over in his mind for days and hadn't able to sleep for nights thinking about it.

I'd heard this sort of thing many times before, as you may imagine, but in this case I was not only extremely disappointed in Frank but justifiably angry. For a start it was a bit late in the day to bring these matters up now, valid though they undoubtedly were. On the other hand I realized his decision must have taken him a considerable amount of moral courage and he must have known I would be furious, apart from his obligations to his unit. The time for resigning was long past. I pointed out to him that by doing so now, at so late a stage, he would be jeopardizing the lives of his men. His second in command was a good chap but not sufficiently experienced to take over at such short notice. Had he thought of that? His resignation in this manner a day or two before we were due to go into battle was totally unreasonable and, worse than that, might also be interpreted by some people as cowardice in the face of the enemy.

Yes, he had thought of all of these things but whatever I said would make no difference. He had made up his mind to go and there was no stopping him. I let him go.

A few days later we assaulted the town of Baraka in an amphibious landing after a 240 kilometre approach up Lake Tanganyika. It was a highly dangerous and complex operation, but one which, if successful, would shorten the war by many months. An amphibious landing is probably the most difficult of all military operations, and more prone to extraneous factors, such as weather, than any other. Casualties were, regrettably, disproportionately high. Frank's second in command, who was also one of the beach reconnaissance party, was killed in the landing. For a few days it was touch and go as to whether we would make it. At one stage it looked as though I might have to evacuate my toe-hold on Baraka, but it turned out well in the end. The fall of Baraka, which had a special significance for the enemy (the Arabic word meaning as it does, 'an enchanted place'), spelt the beginning of the end of the revolution.

Our enemy on this occasion were Cuban mercenary soldiers under the command of Che Guevara, the famous Cuban guerrilla, who had come to Africa to spread the Communist gospel. He didn't succeed in this to any great extent but it could fairly be said that he planted the seed. He returned to

Bolivia shortly after this battle, but his men remained to form the vanguard of almost 120,000 Cuban mercenary soldiers who would be distributed throughout the continent of Africa, mostly in Congo Brazza, Angola and Mozambique, in the years to come.

Some months later I was back at home.

One morning my wife read me a piece from the morning paper at the breakfast table, shock and horror written all over her face. There had been an air pageant at an aerodrome somewhere south of Salisbury, Rhodesia. On show were various types of aircraft, a display of acrobatic flying and so on. A parachute club had made a series of thrilling delayed drops. Frank, who was then living in Rhodesia, had taken his family for the outing. A Dakota DC3 coming in to land had misjudged the distance, overshot the runway and run into a crowd of spectators at the far end of it.

Frank and two of his daughters had been killed instantly.

8

And ... They Were Not Divided

From time to time 5 Commando would be visited by the US military attaché to the American embassy in Léopoldville. Colonel Knut Raudstein was the typical American Army senior officer, sophisticated, knowledgeable and highly articulate. He used his visits to bring himself up to date with what was happening in the mercenary world. We used his visits to bring ourselves up to date with what was happening in the political world of the Congo, and to find out how the various Congolese personalities in Léopoldville were faring in their bid for power.

Another of Knut's reasons for visiting us at Kamina was to check on the presence of any American nationals who might have joined up as mercenary soldiers, unbeknown to the US authorities in Léopoldville. I was always happy to co-operate with Colonel Raudstein in this matter and enjoyed seeing him.

It was generally understood at this time that it was unlawful for an American national to serve as a mercenary soldier anywhere in the world, but on closer examination this was found not to be the entire truth. What was strictly forbidden was for an American national to swear an oath of allegiance to a foreign army, which was not quite the same thing. But to all intents and purposes the difference was unimportant, as the US embassy made strenuous efforts to dissuade any US citizen from serving as a mercenary soldier in the Congo. It was intimated that any American rash enough to flout these instructions would find himself in serious trouble when he got home. Be that as it may, it did not stop a small number of Americans from enlisting as mercenary soldiers in the Congolese National Army. They said they were prepared to accept the consequences, the worst of which appeared to be, at that time, that they might be deprived of their passports, temporarily. So it turned out that from contract to contract I might have four or five Americans in the unit at any one time.

On one occasion I had an American volunteer who called himself Jet. His real name was Jethro Q. Morgenster. With a name like that he had to be an American. Not only an American but an ex-marine. Jet was a quiet man, never drank, never swore, kept himself to himself and attended assiduously to his command of thirty men. He was a thorough professional soldier who delighted in his work. His men admired his competence. Jet was universally popular.

Jacobus Martinus Meyer, on the other hand, was just as obviously an Afrikaaner. The men called him Jake. He was a giant of a man, coarse-grained, rough and tough, immensely loyal once you had won his respect and thoroughly dependable in the worst possible conditions. Off duty he was a hell-raiser and loved his beer. After the third he was prepared to fight any three Englishmen with one hand tied behind his back. He also had a command of thirty men.

What the two men had in common was that they were natural leaders of men. I could never ask for better. That the two should have been drawn towards each other can only be explained by the strange phenomenon known as 'the attraction of opposites'. And in the course of time they became firm friends. Both of them were loners, so that when their contract was ended neither of them returned to South Africa or to Rhodesia but stayed on in the Congo and signed on again. This happened twice, so that by the time the third contract began they were the most experienced men in the unit. Both of them were unmarried and apparently without any relatives or dependants. At any rate they never talked about them.

Off duty Jet and Jake were inseparable. When the unit was in barracks, during the training period prior to action, it was not unusual to see Jet helping the enormous Jake home from some riotous party and, no doubt, putting him to bed with care.

One day I issued the warning order for an operation which would begin in ten days time. Two of the small administrative details which I insisted upon before an action were that every man must wear his dogtag (identity disc) and that his Will should be in order. I was not altogether surprised when I came to check these documents to find that Jake had left whatever he possessed in the world to Jet, and Jet had done the same for Jake. In fact, need I say, neither of them had anything tangible to leave to the other except that one thing – the indemnity which would be paid if he was killed in action. This sum of money he could will to anybody he chose. It was this significant item that each left to the other in the event of death. Neither of them gave it a further thought. That they might be killed in action was something that never entered their heads. Fortunately most soldiers think that way.

Action was joined a few days later, and Jet was killed in an ambush on the Fizi road. As you may imagine, Jake was almost prostrate with grief, so that I allowed him to accompany Jet's body back to Albertville for burial in the cemetery there. Some American Cubans, who were flying our T28s and B26s, provided a guard of honour at the funeral, fired a volley over the grave and flew the Stars and Stripes at half-mast at their camp. I informed Colonel Raudstein as a matter of courtesy.

When the contract ended, Jake decided to return to Johannesburg and told me he would not be coming back again. I could see that he had tried to carry on as usual but in the end he just could not accept the loss of his old friend. Something more precious than he had realized had gone out of his life. I was of course extremely sorry to see him go like this but I was fairly certain that time would make amends and life would go on. Perhaps he would come back if he found it hard to settle down again in civilian life. Meanwhile the indemnity which would come to Jake under Jet's Will might help him start a new life somewhere, or compensate him in some other way. I sincerely hoped so. But it was not to be.

I was on leave when the police rang me up. They had been called to a boarding-house in Mayfair, one of Johannesburg's seedy suburbs, and been asked by the proprietor to break down a door to one of the rooms which he had let to a young man two days previously. The proprietor had reason to believe that all was not well.

Inside the room they found Jake lying on the floor, dead.

To one side of his body five empty bottles of brandy were drawn up in line. In one of his pockets there was a snapshot of himself and Jet in uniform, both laughing. There was also a note addressed to the police.

Under his head was a haversack containing a cheque on the Swiss Bank Corporation, Geneva, Switzerland, for $20,000 US, payable to him by order of the Congolese government.

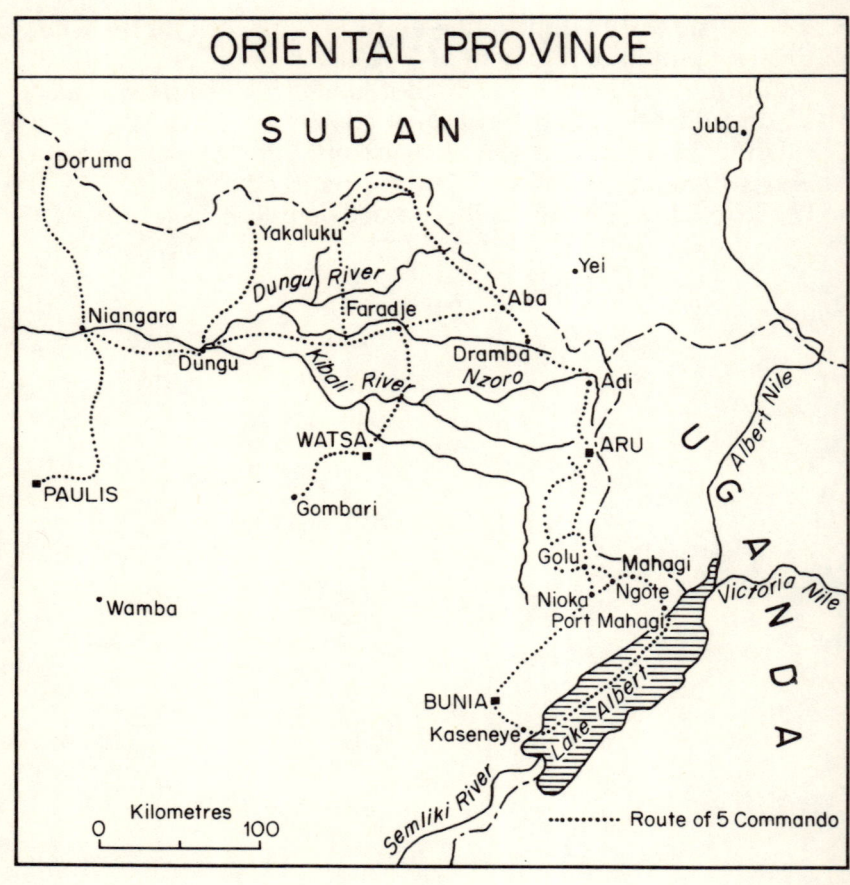

ORIENTAL PROVINCE

S U D A N

Doruma

Juba

Yakaluku

Dungu River

Yei

Niangara

Faradje

Aba

Dungu

Kibali River

Dramba

Nzoro

Adi

WATSA

ARU

Gombari

U

Golu

Mahagi

Nioka

Ngote

Albert Nile

Port Mahagi

PAULIS

Wamba

G

Victoria Nile

A

BUNIA

Lake Albert

N

Kaseneye

D

Semliki River

A

Kilometres

0   100

··········· Route of 5 Commando

9

The Committee Men

My unit was consolidating its position in the north-eastern corner of the Congo. I had set up my headquarters at a place called Faradje, once an Arab slave-trading station on the caravan route from the interior to the Sudan. Wide, red-earth streets ran through the town in shaded avenues, their sides lined with mango trees. Most of these were well over a hundred years old and had been planted by the Arab slavers, so that now they grew in thick profusion. It was late March and the over-ripe fruit littered the ground with a sweet, sickly smell attracting swarms of flies, wasps and bees. Age old-palms dotted the landscape, a multitude of wells testifying mutely to the dryness of the area. In the distance a line of arthritic-looking camels plodded patiently towards the Sudan border.

Sometimes as I walked slowly through the town I would close my eyes and breathe deeply – well, perhaps not too deeply – and transport myself back to the evil days of the slave trade. In my mind's eye I could see an endless file of black men, women and children, yoked together in sad-eyed groups, dragging themselves desperately along these same red roads under the watchful eye of other black men, armed with whips and rifles. Destination the coast, or Zanzibar, or the Upper Nile. Yet for all its history Faradje wasn't a bad place to be stationed in, as such places went in the Congo.

Nothing much was happening on our front at this time other than a threatened visit from the Commander in Chief of the Congolese National Army, Lieutenant-General Joseph-Désiré Mobutu, so that boredom, the arch-enemy of all soldiers, began to blossom. And when boredom blossoms among the *mercenariat*, can villainy be far behind? Not far, as

77

I am going to show you.

But first let me tell you something about Sergeant Samuel Shoesmith, my intelligence sergeant. He was fairly typical of mercenary soldiers under my command at this time, but unique in one respect. He was a Yankee and the only American in 5 Commando on this contract. In fact he was from New York and had his roots in Yonkers. He loved the camaraderie of hard men and the adventure of this type of soldiering where survival depended not so much on rigid routine and formal army training as on the ready acceptance of a necessary discipline, observed willingly by all. He was sharp, astute, fun-loving and easy to get along with. Civilian life he had found weary, stale, flat and mostly unprofitable.

Even so, Sammy knew quite a lot about the business world. In his time he had served behind a counter, been an auctioneer, sold secondhand cars and turned an honest and sometimes a doubtful penny wherever sharp wits and business acumen were in demand. Later he had emigrated hurriedly from the USA to the Northern Rhodesian copperbelt, where a spell in the mines at Luanshya and Kitwe had given him some specialized knowledge concerning high explosives. This he used to his advantage in the Congo whenever the opportunity presented itself. Very soon he became known in 5 Commando as a *fundi* in the use of gelignite and other rapidly expanding substances, particularly those capable of being used in confined spaces. His expertise in this branch of mining was available to all who had occasion to pursue that lucrative if dangerous occupation, always of course for a reasonable consideration.

I had observed on a number of occasions that he was usually the first to be consulted about the validity of banknotes and other negotiable instruments, bills of exchange etc which the men had liberated from banks and post offices unfortunate enough to lie on our general line of advance. 'Ask Sammy!' they all cried. 'Sammy's bound to know if anyone does'. Superimposed on his mischievous nature was an outrageous sense of humour which made him one of the most popular men in the unit. If you are now picturing Sergeant Shoesmith as an easy-going, happy-go-lucky buccaneer without a care in the world, I have sketched his portrait fairly accurately.

My day usually began at 0600 hours, when Sergeant Shoesmith would bring me the signals received during the night. This morning he arrived looking as though he had been run over by the large wheel of a heavy steamroller.

'What happened, Sergeant?'

He found it difficult to reply. His voice was strained and pain-ridden.

'Hit by a Congolese truck, sir'.

'Badly hurt?'

'Can't say,' he went on, hoarsely, 'until I've seen the doctor. I think one or two ribs may be broke and my lungs may be punctured. Coughing up a bit of blood too. Hurts me to laff.'

I made an informed guess as to the nature of the activities which might have led to Sammy's injuries.

'But you don't want to laugh, do you, Sammy?'

'No, sir.'

'Neither would I if I faced a possible charge of looting government property. Not nice those Congolese gaols, Sammy. Twenty-five to a cell, all stinking to high heaven. No mod cons there, you know. Not nice. Not nice at all. Let me know what the doctor says, won't you?'

He ignored the scurrilous innuendo and withdrew, agony in every step.

I was intrigued. Injuries of this type were so unlikely for Sammy that they put me on enquiry. An error of this sort, arising from sheer incompetence, was so completely out of character that it cried out for investigation. He was after all the crown prince of demolition experts. How come this fall from grace? I found out in the end, of course, but it was a few months before the true story filtered through to me.

Later that morning, as usual, I visited the casualty ward. There were no beds, the sick lay on blankets spread on the floor, but the little hospital functioned well in spite of that. Samuel was sitting bolt upright against a wall, immobile, his chest completely encased in plaster of Paris from neck to navel. The medical orderly explained that the doctor had been called away unexpectedly to one of the out-stations to deal with an emergency and that as Sammy was in considerable pain he had diagnosed the trouble himself and done what he could. Actually he said it behoved him to do what he could, which I thought was rather a nice phrase.

Well, OK, what had he diagnosed? Cracked ribs, incipient
bronchitis, *mal de mer*, housemaid's knee etc, etc. He ran on
and on.

'OK, OK,' I said. 'For Pete's sake, stop. I get your drift.'

If there was one thing I had learned from medical orderlies,
it was that a little knowledge could be a deadly boring thing.
So what was his prognosis? Complete recovery in thirty days
if the patient was given total rest. Sounded reasonable.

When the medical officer returned, he endorsed the treat-
ment given by his orderly but with a disbelieving shake of
his head. After further examination of the patient he said it
would be a pity to disturb the art work of his valued assistant,
so he intended to leave well alone. It seemed obvious to him
that the gallant sergeant would be no use to anybody in that
condition and he thought, in the circumstances, it might be
a good thing if Sergeant Shoesmith was granted one month's
sick leave instead of being allowed to lie around there clut-
tering up his hospital making a damn nuisance of himself. I
agreed, so off he went.

After Sammy's departure for Léopoldville and New York,
the true story leaked through to me in dribs and drabs by that
process of osmosis which commanding officers do not encourage but frequently benefit by. In every unit somebody
always spills the beans. The story unfolded in this manner.

The previous night Sammy and two of his buddies were
paying a social visit after dark to an empty house which had
been in better and more settled times the residence of His
Grace the Bishop of Faradje, a Roman Catholic dignitary of
some pre-eminence. In one of the still well-furnished reception rooms they discovered to their astonishment a small oil
painting in an ornate gilt frame which looked to their discern-
ing eyes agreeably rare and valuable. The consensus confirmed that it was a Dutch scene of the seventeenth century.
On closer examination by the art expert, Sergeant Samuel
Shoesmith, none other, it was declared to be a genuine
Rembrandt! If he was not very much mistaken, it was *The
Night Watch*, a reproduction of which had hung in his
mother's front parlour when he was a boy. Or something
very like it at any rate. But rare and valuable without a doubt,
you could take his word for it. The scene certainly depicted
some sort of a guard led by a figure that was, conceivably, an
officer doing his rounds in what could, very easily, be a

narrow street in old Amsterdam. Well, if not Amsterdam, then some city in Holland, certainly.

No sooner was this priceless painting positively identified by the knowledgeable three than it was removed from its valuable frame and secreted athwart Samuel's ample belly, to be covered at once by his camouflage jump jacket.

The warriors then took themselves off to a quieter and safer place far from the inquisitive eyes of the garrison police. A quorum being present, a council of war was convened, presided over by Chairman Sammy. For this purpose he transformed himself in the twinkling of an eye from a harmless intelligence sergeant into a suave and sophisticated Fifth Avenue art-dealer. It says something for the strength of Sammy's personality, or the powers of self-deception, that this improbable metamorphosis passed completely unnoticed by the members of the committee, neither of whom was privy to the fact that Sammy's total acquaintance with the world of fine art rested precariously on the strength of one visit he had paid to an art gallery many years before, under the impression, erroneous, that some live models, female, were to be on display in the nude.

Certain things have a present value, as any actuary, or stockbroker, or Sammy, could have told them. In fact Sammy went on to tell them just that, that the present value of an oil painting, no matter how rare and valuable as this one undoubtedly was, in a place like Faradje and in circumstances like theirs, when converted into Congolese francs was as near as dammit to a big zero. His expert opinion was that if a willing buyer for the painting could be found in Faradje at this moment, the proceeds would not have bought them a small glass of beer apiece, even at the most optimistic estimate. True, a bottle of Johnny Walker had been auctioned by Sammy in a barrack room for a paltry $183 US on the eve of battle some weeks ago, which said something for the economic theory of supply and demand, but an oil painting, now, that was different, that called for an appreciation by the *cognoscenti*. Any man in his right senses could see at a glance how valuable the thing was and sell it for hundreds of thousands of dollars US in an appreciative market. But here, in this godforsaken spot! He shrugged off the thought. Philistines, ignorant bums, said Mr Samuel Shoesmith, art-dealer, with a sniff of disdain, no, no, that was completely beyond their comprehension. A bitterness foreign to Sammy's sunny disposition began to contaminate his normally happy little soul.

The committee men began to deliberate. An hour later the acidity of their blood-count began to rise steeply. The gross injustice of their situation permeated their being. It hardly bore thinking about. Here they were, sitting on a gold mine, only to be separated from a willing and lucrative market by about 3,000 kilometres of assorted African jungle, give or take a hundred kilometres or so. Just their bleeding luck.

It was then that Sammy produced the palm toddy, the golden elixir from which all inspiration is known to spring in darkest Africa. And spring it did. After copious libations the solution became increasingly obvious. One of them must get back pronto to the fleshpots of New York, New York, with the priceless work of art secreted about his person. But how? Compassionate leave? No good asking the CO who was known to be a thorough-going bastard and as hard as nails. Their chances in that direction were less than nil. No, the only solution, obvious when they stopped to think about it, was for one of them to get wounded in action and get invalided out, taking the merchandise with him. The snag about that was that there was no action going on at the moment, so a convenient wound was not really a feasible plan. They cogitated. What about a serious injury then? Of course, every bit as good. One of them could get run down by a Congolese ration truck! Just the thing, and how probable. That sort of thing happened every day, didn't it? But no, that solution, good though it was, wouldn't give them the control over the type of injuries they thought their agent should bear. That led them to consider precisely what injuries were most likely to carry conviction.

Sammy suggested breaking an arm or a leg – not his, of course – but this idea, rather close to home, seemed to find little favour with the other members of the committee. Then they approached the plan from a different angle. Who was to be their chosen representative? Who was to bear the noble stigmata? A majority of two had little difficulty in arriving at a conclusion. The only man with that deep knowledge of art and the sophistication necessary to convince a purchaser of the value of their merchandise was Sammy, so Samuel would have to be a brave little Sammy and go. And if injuries were necessary to convince the MO, Sammy would have to grin and bear them for the common weal. One of the committee men had read something somewhere about one suffering for all and was entirely in favour of that idea, providing he wasn't the single sufferer, of course. History, he said, was full of examples like that, wasn't it? It was, but that didn't stop the chairman from casting a dissenting vote.

But with the passage of time and liquor Sammy began to see himself in a dim heroic light, a martyr to the cause, when happily it occurred to his agile brain that injuries and pain and all that rotten stuff were totally unnecessary. Surely he could kid on at sick parade that he was stricken with some virulent disease? The stinking Congo was full of them. Take your pick. But which one? And how could Sammy convince the medical officer he was mortally ill and in dire need of prolonged sick leave? That was the question. Sammy Hamlet, racked with indecision and clothed now in a black velvet suit with a thin rapier by his side, began to intone a half-remembered soliloquy, forgot the words, thought better of it and downed another pint of rotgut instead.

Another hour, another gourd of toddy and the whole thing became ridiculously simple. A plan gelled. Bring Nobby Clark into the swindle. Nobby was just the man they needed, a reliable villain. Nobby was the MO's orderly. He had a corner in valium and welconal which he guarded zealously, and knew how to keep his trap shut. A crafty man of infinite cunning.

Nobby must arrange for the doctor to be called away for a visit first thing tomorrow morning before sick parade so that Nobby would have to take the parade himself. Sammy would pretend he had some broken ribs, a misplaced sternum and an enlarged if not septic spleen, things they knew about vaguely that occurred somewhere between the neck and the belly button. Nobby would then place valuable oil painting against Sammy's skin and cover same with plaster of Paris. Perform caesarean operation in New York, extract canvas baby and sell for an independent fortune. What a plan! Split the proceeds four ways, or thereabouts, mused Sammy, a little ahead of the others in that. Nothing short of genius. This way there would be no trouble with the Congolese customs or the customs at Kennedy Airport either. Brilliant. Minds like theirs were wasted in a god-forsaken hole like Faradje. They had another calabash of palm wine to celebrate the discovery.

Fortuitously the night ended in an almighty barney during which the hapless Sammy got himself well and truly worked over by the other two members of the committee, who had become unreasonably argumentative, for no apparent reason other than the three gallons of toddy they had consumed. In the ensuing punch-up a spectacular damage was done to Sammy's ribs, two of which appeared to be cracked if not actually broken. It answered all their prayers. If that wasn't the hand of God moving in His mysterious ways, they'd like to know, what was?

Nobby was squared, the MO was given the bogus message, and Sergeant Samuel Shoesmith, the victim of a dastardly hit-and-run accident, perpetrator unknown, got his sick leave.

I only wish I could have been present when the elegant Mr Shoesmith emerged from his cocoon in the Taft Hotel just off Broadway near Times Square. Truth to tell, the plaster of Paris cocoon, now somewhat blackened by usage and a hundred ribald autographs, had been giving him all the tortures of hell. He had a hairy chest, and everything from adventurous breadcrumbs to tiny equatorial insects had invaded the warm and inviting darkness between the plaster and his skin, tormenting him beyond all endurance and causing him to prance around from time to time like a whirling dervish. In a flash Sammy had cleaned off his outer casing, resuscitated the oil painting, mounted it suitably in another gilt frame and trotted round nonchalantly to meet with Mr Abraham Z. Rubenstein, the famous New York art critic and dealer in Works of Fine Art, Ming China, *objets d'art* etc on Fifth Avenue.

'You say you have a Rembrandt for me to see, Mr Shoesmith?' began Mr Rubenstein evenly, without any visible display of emotion, while balancing a pair of gold-rimmed pince-nez on the end of his nose. 'Most interesting, most interesting. Which one might it be, may I ask? And what of its provenance?'

Sammy side-stepped that one, which was only right and proper, given that he had never heard that word before in his life, never mind understood it.

'I'm pretty certain its the *Night Watch*, Mr. Rubenstein,'

said our hero confidently, who lacked not in poise, even in this arcane field.

'*Night Watch, Night Watch, Night Watch,*' murmured Mr. Rubenstein to himself, moistening a finger as he paged rapidly through a thick catalogue of paintings by the old masters. 'Ah, yes. Here we are. *Night Watch.* Rembrandt. Four metres by three. Presently in the Rijksmuseum in Amsterdam ...'

A lesser man than Sammy would have been nonplussed, possibly mortified, but not our Samuel.

'Yes, yes, of course, I know that, Mr Rubenstein. But this is a miniature by the same artist, er, isn't it? You know, they sometimes did a small one first just to get their hand in, didn't they? Must be worth a few grand?'

'Well, yes. Everything is possible.'

Mr Rubenstein examined the canvas closely with a magnifying glass. Turned it over and removed the backing. Some faded chalk marks and mummified insects testified to the age of the work. Sammy could tell the expert was vastly impressed. Probably figuring to himself what sort of a six-figure fortune he could get for it at Sotheby's. Sammy held his breath as visions of race tracks, five-star hotels and obliging girls passed rapidly in glorious succession before his eyes.

Mr Rubenstein was a kind old man who had seen it all before in a long and distinguished career. He spread a small safety net.

'At a generous estimate, Mr Shoesmith, I would say $20 for the painting and', catching sight of Sammy's crestfallen face, 'maybe $30 for the frame.'

Sammy felt as though someone had switched off the sunlight at its source. His unconquerable spirit sagged. But he rallied. He walked slowly up Fifth Avenue with the Rembrandt held loosely under his arm. What the hell, he said to himself, tomorrow's another day. He stopped outside St Patrick's and stuffed the painting into a trash can. Suddenly he felt an unaccountable yearning for the mango-treed avenues of far-off Faradje, the peaceful savannah of the Sudan border, and the uncomplicated company of his partners in crime, his loyal mates, the committee men.

10
Hans Germani

Lieutenant Hans Germani was a genius. I don't mean in the military context, particularly, although in his way he was an exceptional soldier too. Exceptionally untidy, exceptionally hungry and exceptionally courageous. He had a distressing habit of standing on the leading armoured car as it approached an enemy position, holding on to the turret with one hand and firing his Vigneron from the hip with the other. I had to restrain him in the end. As I often said to him, a bullet-proof German officer has yet to be invented.

He was my intelligence officer, and in this field he was outstanding. At interrogation of prisoners he was brilliant, penetrating and persuasive, never finding it necessary to beat the life out of any of them. He could speak seven European languages fluently and go from one to another in the same sentence without a pause. He also spoke Swahili and one or two of the East African dialects. His English vocabulary was extensive and certainly much greater than mine. While he never managed a faultless English accent, the only words which gave him difficulties were 'clothes' and 'months', which became 'clotheses' and 'monthses'. He had a mastery of English idiom second to none. He was the only foreigner I have ever met who could explain the Latin tag *'post hoc, ergo propter hoc'* in simple English.

He was fourteen years of age when World War II was drawing to a close in Germany. He was one of that gallant band of boy soldiers who were pressed into service by the Wehrmacht at the eleventh hour, in a last desperate bid to stem the advance of the American and British armies on Berlin. Perhaps one of the most heart-rending and poignant episodes of the war. Nobody likes fighting against children.

After he was demobilized he became a medical student in Frankfurt and qualified as a doctor seven years later. He emigrated to Kenya, gave up his career in medicine and became foreign correspondent in Africa for the prestigious German newspaper *Die Bild*. But it was not his adventurous background nor his academic qualifications which attracted me most. For me the most magnetic thing about Hans was his wonderful sense of humour. This is an example.

Captain K had been a disaster. As an infantry officer he had been an unmitigated failure. In the field he attracted calamity like iron filings to a magnet. In administrative posts he became a veritable vortex of certain chaos. These types exist; one just has to avoid them, not employ them. In desperation I had posted him to Léopoldville to be 5 Commando liaison officer with Congolese National Army headquarters. Not that this posting was in any way a sinecure but at least he spoke reasonable schoolboy French and some Swahili and was generally of an inoffensive demeanour. But even in this comparatively harmless role he had managed to screw things up and scatter confusion far and wide.

We were in the middle of a battle near Watsa in Oriental Province when I received tidings of his latest *bêtise*, accompanied by a friendly letter from General Bobozo, the C-in-C, that intimated the Congo would be a happier place without his services. It was more than a hint; it was a directive. This was the final straw. I had to do something drastic. I sent for Lieutenant Germani.

'Hans!'

'*Herr Kolonel*.' Hans clicked his heels. He knew I liked that.

'Hans, send a signal to Léo. Address it to Captain K, care of QG, information paymaster etc etc; you know the distribution. Tell Captain K he's fired as of now and to get the hell out of it within forty-eight hours.'

A few minutes later Hans returned with a signal pad and a message ready for signature. It read:

YOUR CONTRACT TERMINATES ON RECEIPT THIS SIGNAL STOP DEPART CONGO WITHIN 48 HOURS STOP ABUSIVE LETTER FOLLOWS STOP OC 5 COMMANDO.

11
The Puritan

There are two ways of really getting to know a man. One is to go to sea with him in a small boat, the other is to soldier with him in action. As I had served with Sergeant Major Brady for more than a year, much of it in action, I was entitled to say I really knew him, probably even better than his mother. If he ever had one, which I doubted from time to time.

Jim Brady was a puritan, although I don't think he would have recognized himself as such. He was upright, humourless and correct. But above all he was reliable, efficient and superbly self-disciplined. And those characteristics in a soldier are pearls without price. I often told him he would have been a natural for the *Mayflower* in 1620. He even looked a bit like a Pilgrim Father, except he was clean-shaven. If he had missed the boat at Plymouth Rock, I felt sure Oliver Cromwell would have recruited him gladly for his model army some forty years later.

RSM Brady had impressed me in a number of ways. He began and ended each day with a quarter of an hour's reading from the Bible, no matter what the situation. I am sure he knew his Bible thoroughly, but unlike most of those who do, especially soldiers, he never bent your ear with quotations from the scriptures. Neither did he discuss Christianity or religion with me or anybody else. His beliefs were strictly personal. Evangelism was not a part of his make-up. Calvinism, I suspected, was the ruling power in his life, but I doubt if he derived much spiritual solace from the practice of its forbidding doctrine. He set a high standard of discipline for the men and applied the same standard to himself. The net effect of this was to make him aloof and unapproachable.

He was not the sort of man you could take your problems to. He existed on a different and more rarefied plane. But on a purely professional level he was a superb soldier. His turn-out was impeccable, even in the midst of battle. He had a strange habit of carrying around with him seven complete uniforms, one for each day of the week. He employed a Congolese orderly who kept his kit in spotless condition, and paid him privately out of his own pocket. His boots weren't just clean, they shone. But apart from that, one of the things which impressed me most about him was his unchanging attitude towards the men. Hard but reasonable. Better than that, it was consistent. They knew exactly where they stood with him at all times. He courted no popularity and didn't need to. A gem of a warrant officer, and I really thought I knew him. But one day he surprised me.

My unit was in the Oriental province of the Congo, the one in the top right-hand corner of the map, where the border marches with Uganda and the Sudan. The rebels in Oriental were being supplied at an estimated rate of thirty tons of hardware per day, most of it of Soviet origin, coming up the Nile and finding its way via Juba and Yei across the Congo border to Aba and Faradje. Quite a lot of stuff was coming also from Uganda, across the border at Aru. Our next campaign against the rebels was designed to extinguish this line of supply. But we must start in the Lake Albert area. The capture of Port Mahagi, at its northern end, was a tactical necessity before our general advance in a westerly direction could begin. Our right flank must be secured first.

But there were tactical problems to solve before we could begin our planned advance. This part of the country was extremely heavily populated, in places the villages running into each other for miles on end. Furthermore we were uncertain as to how deeply Communist propaganda had penetrated, or what kind of reception we might expect from the ordinary villagers. Information of this type was vital. If we found that the population was solidly against us and in favour of the rebel movement, we must conclude that the politicians directing our actions had made an error. In that event negotiation, not war, was more likely to be the right answer. On the other hand if the population regarded us as a liberating force, we would succeed. In this case they would assist us, and their support would make all the difference. So it became vital for us to get some reliable knowledge of the attitude of the local population in the first place, and then to find the strength and locality of the enemy in the second. At this stage we had no reliable information about either. We would be obliged to gather and evaluate it ourselves. The evaluation process was already in the capable hands of Hans Germani, my intelligence officer, a German medical doctor turned soldier who spoke Swahili fluently and one or two of the local dialects as well.

But the information gathering-process would not be quite so simple. Armoured car patrols supported by trucked infantry would more than likely scare the villagers deep into the bush. Our tactics would have to be more subtle than that. Peaceful contact was the keynote. To this end I sought the support of the local chiefs. I soon discovered that they were sick to death with the high-handed way in which the Armée Populaire de Libération, the rebel army, had taken over the area. Rapine and murder committed by the rebels were commonplace. Discipline among their forces was non-existent, but the man with the gun was king and could demand whatever he wanted from the frightened villagers. In practice they were forced to supply the rebel army with everything from blankets and food to porters and women. So that when I asked the chiefs and notables for men whom we could train as scouts for the purpose of getting information they offered them to me readily.

In a few days we had raised a small force of about one hundred young men, fit and eager to bring in all the information we needed. If they were to confront the enemy, they must be able to protect themselves, so to this end I provided them with some elementary military training. I brought them under the personal supervision of Lieutenant Germani for this purpose. Hans enjoyed his command. Now he saw himself as General von Lettow-Vorbeck, the German commander who had given the British Army the run-around in East Africa during the First World War, the famous general who never knew defeat but was no stranger to victory. Hans called his Askari warriors 'the Black Watch'. Somebody else called them the Queen's Own Mobutu Highlanders. They were armed with everything from bows and arrows to ancient Martini Henry shotguns (pou-pous), which I would have treated with the greatest suspicion before firing, but their owners seemed to love them with a passion. I supplemented these arms with some pre-Great War bolt-action Mausers, possibly the finest single-round military rifle of all time, better in my view than the American Ross or P14, and even the early British Lee Enfields.

One group of the new scout force was led by a handsome young lad of eighteen. He was the grand chief's son and the obvious choice as commander. When I first met him I remarked on his splendid physique and dignified bearing. He was wearing a white steel helmet, US Army pattern, the chinstraps hanging free in the approved romantic manner. After we had exchanged courtesies I began. Hans Germani interpreted for me in Swahili.

'Hans,' I said, 'tell Handsome Harry (for such I had named him) I would prefer it if he did not wear that white steel helmet. Explain why. The rebels, especially their military police, often wear white steel helmets and it is possible our men might mistake him for a rebel one night in the dark.'

Handsome Harry was upset. The helmet was not just a head-covering, it was also some sort of status symbol, something which conferred on him an aura of authority in the eyes of his followers. It was his heraldic shield, no less. So we compromised. We agreed that he could wear the helmet at all times except when on patrol or when he was likely to come into contact with the enemy. Now he was happy.

The brigade, which I commanded, was now able to move forward on two axes, the reconnaissance section commanded by the chief's son under Lieutenant Germani providing a forward screen for my column. We advanced slowly, testing the strength of the rebel army as we went. Day by day the scouts brought back valuable information regarding enemy dispositions and the reactions of the population, which Hans processed swiftly, building up a favourable picture.

One night, just as it was getting dark, Hans told me that all indications now pointed to one thing: the enemy must be in considerable strength in a town about fifteen kilometres away, with a strongly held outpost about three kilometres down the road from our present position. The road was only a ribbon of earth carved out of the flat countryside, with a shallow ditch on either side of it, and at this point ran dead straight as far as the eye could see.

As night fell I brought a platoon of 81 mm mortars into action and plastered the road ahead of the enemy's estimated position. This was intended solely to frighten the defenders off and leave the road to us. During the night I could concentrate sufficient force to advance on the main enemy position by day. The idea of an actual engagement in the dark was something I would never entertain. We just didn't have the training for that most difficult of all manoeuvres. From past experience I knew the bombardment would do the trick. The enemy would abandon the position and withdraw hastily, probably two or three miles down the road, where they would set up another position.

The bombardment ceased and after a short pause I got Hans to send out a patrol of the Black Watch to see if the enemy had gone. It was commanded by Handsome Harry.

About the time that they were due back Sergeant Major Brady and I made our way to the most forward position and awaited their return. We took cover in a field close by, from which we could see every detail of the road ahead. Half an hour later the moon got up and bathed the scene in a silvery light, strong enough to cast solid black shadows on the sandy white road. It was dead quiet. Nothing stirred. The recce patrol was due back at any minute by my reckoning and would give a recognition signal, the usual drill, before rejoining our lines. But nothing happened. I was beginning to wonder if they had hit trouble, an ambush perhaps, but dismissed it as unlikely. Surely we would have heard something in the quiet of the night if they had. I dismissed the possibility.

Another hour passed. I was getting more than a little apprehensive when suddenly Brady nudged me and pointed down the road. I could just make out a group of figures about 150 metres away, hurrying towards us furtively, in complete silence, keeping in the shadows as they ran. As they got nearer we could see quite clearly that the leader of the group was wearing a white helmet. Unlikely, I figured, but they could be an enemy patrol. Sergeant Major Brady raised his FN and drew a bead on the man in the white helmet. I made a move to depress the barrel.

'Hold it, Jim, for Pete's sake. It might be … '

Too late. Brady pressed the trigger. Crack! The single shot

blasted out. The leading figure dropped in his tracks. The remainder of the group screamed out the password as the shot echoed down the column. We ran forward to meet them.

The sergeant major turned the body over with his foot. It was the grand chief's son. Handsome Harry was stone dead, blood pouring from his white helmet.

'God forgive us, Jim!' I said quietly to the sergeant major, and then ordered some men to carry the body back into our lines. Brady went with it, head down and silent.

During the next hour or so while I was busy deploying the column for the night, my thoughts kept harking back to the tragedy. To kill a man, your ally, your friend, by mistake was the most damnable thing that could happen to a soldier. Even the most insensitive man would lash himself with remorse and recrimination. I wondered how Brady was taking it. I imagined he must be feeling he was to blame and hating himself for it. I could understand that. I would have to help him through that dark passage, if I could.

After I had checked that all sentries were posted and the column settled down for the night, I made my way back to my headquarters. Jim was sitting on a box of .762 mm ammunition drinking a mug of C-ration cocoa. In the background his orderly was polishing his boots. Behind him was his Friday uniform, already laid out for the morrow. I avoided his eyes.

'If it makes you feel any better, Jim,' I began, 'it was obviously a mistake. Anyone could have made it.'

He looked up in surprise and laughed, as though he had just caught on to what I was saying.

'Oh, him! Silly muggins. Shouldn't have worn that stupid helmet. Only got himself to blame. I heard you telling him not to, several times ... '

The Sergeant Major shrugged his shoulders. He had dismissed the whole episode from his mind. Like Handsome Harry it had ceased to exist.

'What time are you giving out orders for tomorrow, sir?' he asked.

12
Gangala-Na-Bodio

An army, said Napoleon, or so we are reliably informed, marches on its stomach. There are no truer words in the annals of military affairs than these. Anybody who has had even the slightest brush with the planning of a campaign, particularly an advance into enemy territory, will recognize the truth of them. It is a truism that no campaign can begin until the logistics of supply are solved. How to feed and water your men, for example, is probably the most important initial requirement and one which finds its way down to even the humblest command. It is a constant in every plan, a pre-requisite to any operation and very often a quartermaster's nightmare.

In this connection the story of Colonel William Hicks of the Bombay Army will repay a moment's thought. Colonel Hicks was the commander of the Egyptian force dispatched up the Nile in 1883 to subdue the Mahdi, the new incarnation of the Prophet. The Mahdi had established himself in the Kordofan province of the Sudan at El Obeid, a city he had captured after months of siege. A *jihad*, a holy war, was in the making, and the Egyptian government, who held sway over the Sudan, was fearful of the outcome. The Mahdi must be put down before he became too powerful. The colonel, together with his staff of a dozen or so European officers, plus two journalists (the press, like the poor, are always with us!), rode out of Cairo bound for the Sudan at the head of 7,000 Egyptian and Sudanese infantry, 1,000 cavalry and about 2,000 camp-followers. More than 5,000 camels were needed to transport their supplies across the desert and to carry their mountain and machine-guns, plus a million rounds of ammunition. A formidable baggage train.

In his magnificent book *The White Nile* Alan Moorehead says, 'Colonel Hicks was a thorough going British officer who was not at all lacking in courage, and he might have done very well had he been leading an expedition in Europe. But this was Africa.'

Humbly, I draw your attention to those last four words.

The expedition reached Khartoum in good order and then a place 160 kilometres farther up the Nile, from whence they marched westwards across the dry plains, for some 250 kilometres, making for El Obeid. Within days of their sojourn in the desert, disaster struck Hick's column. The commissariat was inadequate, the supply of water virtually non-existent, and the soldiers were, not surprisingly, unwilling to march.

Meanwhile from El Obeid the Mahdi and his khalifas watched the approach of this cumbersome and helpless column with a predatory joy. Long before the inevitable end there was a despairing note in the dispatches which Hicks sent back to Khartoum: the water had failed, the men and the camels were dying every day, the Mahdi's horsemen had cut off his line of supply to the Nile and, worst of all, he was lost. On 5 November 1883 the expedition was wandering in the depths of a dry forest fifty kilometres to the south of El Obeid, when out of the dawn 50,000 Arab warriors burst upon the stricken column. In the hand-to-hand fighting which followed Hicks' force of 10,000 men was annihilated. The colonel and his European staff perished by the sword. Of the entire force only 300 survived to carry the news back to Cairo.

Napoleon, we are reliably informed again, took steps to overcome the problem of feeding his troops. He offered a substantial prize to the inventor of any means of preserving food in a readily portable fashion. Canned food was the answer. It was used for the first time in the advance on Moscow and eased the problems of supply thereafter.

In World War I the vast armies facing each other in France subsisted basically on canned meat, the famous bully, biscuits and plum jam. In World War II the genius of the American food industry produced in a flash of inspiration the K-ration, to be followed swiftly by the C-ration. Out of respect for those geniuses I will draw a discreet veil over their other creations, Soya Links and Spam. But the C- and K-rations went a long way towards solving one of the quarter-masters' greatest problems. These rations, unlike fresh and frozen foods, could be stored in bulk indefinitely. In addition to this inestimable advantage, the rations were easy to trans-port and could be issued on an individual basis, without the necessity for breaking bulk.

In the Congo, when on campaign, we were always sup-plied with the US Army C-ration. Some of these were, regret-tably, many years old and way past their date of expiry. Some sharp character somewhere was making a killing, I sup-posed, but even so they were still edible. We found that after fourteen days or so the sameness of the diet began to pall, but as a basic ration, to be supplemented by judicious local foraging, it proved unbeatable.

In my unit the ration allowance came in the shape of a cardboard box containing one week's supply for one man. In theory that was the end of the quartermaster's responsibility for the next seven days. In practice, the men tended to eat the next few days' allowance in advance, or were profligate, or generous, or just plain stupid with it. On many occasions I saw members of the Congolese National Army open their rations for the day, select a small tin of fruit salad or pecan nut cake, my favourite, and fling the rest of the box into the bush! From time to time I would give them a small lecture about the wastefulness of their behaviour, and remind them of the cost of these rations, which, incidentally, was hid-eously expensive, but it always failed to impress them. Sol-diers, as a general rule, have little concept of the cost of their maintenance.

(In a completely different, but no less costly, direction there was another slovenly practice which angered me more than somewhat. And that was to see a man fire a long burst from his FN with the sole purpose, as he would admit on being challenged, of cleaning the barrel of his rifle! Eleven or twelve rounds at 25 cents per round, maybe more, not to mention the problems involved in getting them from base to front line, just to do something which a piece of four-by-two flannelette and a pull-through could have done in five min-utes. War has got to be the most wasteful activity of the present age.)

I insisted that junior leaders should form small messes, pool their C-rations, appoint one of their men as cook, forage for fresh vegetables and produce hot meals daily without fail. The result, in terms of morale-building alone, was rewarding and fostered that spirit of camaraderie and self-reliance which is the soul of small-unit warfare. The poor leader, on the other hand, who allows his men to open tins and scoop out unappetizing cold meals, of a sort, will wonder why his men are unhappy with their food. Their performance will suffer accordingly.

Standards in the victualling of armies vary quite markedly from nation to nation, but you may be sure the French soldier will always get his daily litre of *vin ordinaire*, no matter what the circumstances. While I would have been happy to be a *poilu*, I was glad I wasn't a Japanese soldier. During their advance from Burma into Assam, in 1944 at Imphal and Kohima, they thought nothing of exisiting for weeks on end on a simple diet of rice. This was boiled and compacted into the hollow part of the female bamboo, about eight inches long and three wide, which was easy to carry. But then they were unbelievably tough hombres. Of all the armies in the last world war there can be little doubt that GI Joe was the best-fed soldier of all.

In the Congo we didn't do too badly either. The Belgians, who love their grub, saw to that. But sometimes the ration truck bringing the next issue of C-rations to my unit would be delayed. On occasion it might even be ambushed. This fell clutch of circumstance occurred once when we were on the Sudan border. It was partly my fault. I had allowed my line of communication to be stretched dangerously thin, so that we were now about 230 kilometres from our base at Aru, much of it passing through disputed territory. I had relied on an air drop but the weather had closed in on us unexpectedly, making supply by air impossible.

Alistair Wicks, my second in command, who was normally in charge of this side of affairs, was on leave. So I sent for Hans Germani, my intelligence officer. Food was a subject near and dear to his heart.

'Hans,' I began, 'we've only got enough rations for two days. If we don't get a drop or resupply within forty-eight hours we shall have to appoint a commission of foragers to go out and bring in whatever they can to feed the men.'

The notion of a commission of foragers appealed greatly to Hans, who was widely read on matters military. He said it was exactly how the Confederate Army supplied their troops in the American Civil War. I think he saw himself as the officer commanding the commission, with control over all sorts of good things to eat. But after a little study he agreed the foraging party was not really a viable solution in this remote corner of the world. Apart from coffee plantations, palm trees without number, fields of manioc and a few wild horses, the local countryside did not look too promising. Cattle had long since gone the way of all flesh. Living off the land might be feasible for a few men for a day or two, but as a means of sustaining 275 fighting men in the manner to which they had become accustomed it was plainly not a proposition.

'Any other ideas, Hans?'

Germani was a mine of information.

'Do you know about Gangala-Na-Bodio?' he asked.

The name had a pleasant ring about it but beyond that meant nothing to me.

'But you must have heard of the Garamba National Park?'

Of course, the game reserve was unique in Africa and famous throughout the world for the variety of its wildlife. I had heard of the park before and knew it to be exceptional in a number of ways. For one thing, cars were not allowed into it, and visitors had to travel on horseback to view the game.

Hans said he would do some research in the bishop's library and then put up a plan to overcome all our feeding problems. He said it with confidence, clicked his heels and bowed from the waist in the best Prussian High Command manner, which he knew always impressed me. It seemed so right, so inexpressibly German. All he needed to complete the picture was his *pickelhaube*, which, sadly, was missing. But once more, fortunately, my instinct was unerring. In matters of food you can always trust a German soldier.

Hans was no exception. Some hours later he laid his appreciation before me. It was brilliantly executed. It contained the following nuggets of hard information:

The Garamba National Park was situated some forty kilometres west of Faradje, our present station, and was just north of the road to Dungu. It had been established in 1927 and contained giraffe, kudu, waterbuck, hartebeeste, buffalo, lions, many white rhino and, most important of all, thousands of elephants. Hans went on to explain that 'white rhino' was the name given to the square-lipped rhino, almost extinct in Africa today. The rhino was not white but black, like all other rhinos. There were thought to be about sixty to eighty of these lads in the park.

I thanked Hans for this piece of gratuitous information, well known to every schoolboy in southern Africa, and we went on.

The elephants were the chief attraction and glory of the game reserve. It had the unique distinction of being the only place in the whole of the African continent in which elephants were trained to work. Like the ones in Burma and India, I supposed.

The park itself was over a million acres in extent and stretched northwards from the main camp, a place called Gangala-Na-Bodio, to the Sudan border. The terrain, which was mostly savannah and sand, continued in its virgin state right across the north African deserts for over 2,400 kilometres, as far as the Mediterranean. In this vast area were some of the last truly primeval lands in the world. Here the destructive hand of man had made no inroads on nature, and wildlife reigned supreme, exactly as it had since the dawn of time. That was an arresting thought.

'Is it popular as a tourist attraction? Do many people come from all over the world to visit the park?' I asked.

'Indeed they do – or did, until the rebellion. But its remoteness seems to have restricted the number of visitors in the past. And of course it is a bit rugged for those who would prefer to pay for luxury. There are only two camps, one at Gangala and the other about fifty kilometres north of it, at a place called Nagero. To get to Nagero you have to cross the Dungu, a wide river running through the camp at Gangala-Na-Bodio. There is no ferry across this river, other than a primitive raft which is not strong enough to take a motor vehicle. Visitors to the park must go on horseback to watch the animals. Horses and trained guides are available, of course.'

Sounded great to me. But what had this to do with our most pressing need – *nourriture*, as the Belgians said, or grub, as we said.

'Suggested plan of action, as follows,' continued Hans, now a staff officer in Rommel's Afrika Korps. 'We arrive at

Gangala-Na-Bodio, ingratiate ourselves with the game war-
dens in the first case, or rough them up in the second, as
required. Either way we persuade them to go out and shoot
us enough game to restock the larder and feed our famished
soldiery.'

Shoot animals in a game reserve! I registered abject horror.
I had never heard of such a vile, preposterous, cold-blooded,
intelligent solution to all our problems. I gave it all of five
seconds thought.

'Let the wagons roll,' I said.

For a number of reasons it was two days before we reached
Gangala-Na-Bodio. Our normal C-rations were exhausted.
The men, as always, were famished. They made no bones
about it and meant me to know they were ravenously hungry. Men began eyeing each other's proportions with meaningful glances in my presence.

On arrival at Gangala-Na-Bodio a deputation came to see
me. It was ten o'clock in the morning. Their spokesman, an
Italian from Rome – I think his name was Cassius; anyway
he had a lean and hungry look – said, with genuine tears in
his eyes, that the men hadn't eaten a thing since breakfast,
which had ended all of two hours before. I sympathized with
them. I knew how they must be suffering, poor dears. I
promised to do what I could.

We came to a whitewashed stone cottage with a thatched
roof. The column halted. It was the entrance to the Garamba
National Park. Just being here was thrill enough for me. It
was, and is once more, I am happy to say, one of the finest
natural game parks in the world. I had been in my recent past
a hunter, a wildlife enthusiast, a conservationist and later an
honorary game warden in Ngamiland, one of the last natural
wildlife sanctuaries in Africa. But the bellies of my men were
rumbling audibly and I was obliged to do something about
that, and that right speedily.

There were no Belgians among those present. The camp
was being run by a senior game warden, a Congolese named
Enoch Kitale. I questioned him first of all about the presence
of rebels. It seemed logical to me that such a place would be
a natural hide-out for the rebel army, but to my surprise
Kitale told me, truthfully, that there were no rebel camps
anywhere in the reserve. I then laid my problems at his feet
and asked him to help us if he could. He laughed. Of course

he could help, nothing simpler. Just follow me, he said.

We walked a few hundred metres through the camp until we came to the edge of the Dungu river. It was running deep and swiftly, and about seventy metres wide at this point. Putting his hands to his mouth he sang out a long, melodious call which hung on the thin, hot air a brief moment before it withered away to die in the distance. Nothing happened. He did it again, and again. Suddenly the bush on the other side of the river began to quiver as though it had come alive. One by one a string of elephants emerged from the deep bush to stand silently on the sandy track leading down to the river, as though awaiting further orders.

'*Voilà, mes amis,*' said Enoch.

Kitale shouted orders to them in a language they appeared to understand. The elephants ambled slowly down to the water's edge and swam across the river. As they emerged they squirted themselves playfully with water and then gathered around the game guards and me. There were eight of them altogether. They were a bit too close for my comfort and I hoped Kitale had them under proper control.

'And now,' he said, 'we must arrange a small safari.'

'You mean a hunting party?'

'Of course. About sixteen men, two to each elephant. You must come too; I want you to control your men. You and I can go on the leading elephant or on horses, whichever you prefer.'

He pointed to two splendid Arab steeds standing in the shade close by, whisking their tails vigorously. I let him know a horse would suit my leg span better.

'But what are we going to shoot?'

'Buffalo will be the best. They are in splendid condition at the moment. Some of them will weigh more than 400 kilos! Don't worry. We have large herds of them and in any case they need culling. It's two years since anyone came here to check on their numbers, but I know, I see them every day.'

'But what shall we shoot them with?'

'You've got rifles, haven't you?'

'Yes' I said, 'of course. But they are army rifles! Point 762 mm!'

The idea of shooting game with an FN rifle was barbaric. Why that should be, I can't really figure out, but that's how I felt at the time. I made a grimace. But Hans couldn't see what all the fuss was about.

'With respect, sir. The men need food. May we please get on with it before night falls? It may take six hours or more to bring in enough meat for the column.'

I called for volunteers for the shooting party. Over a hundred gathered round me in an instant. I chose fourteen men, most of whom said they were greatly experienced big game hunters. Some, seeking vicarious fame, claimed they had hunted big game in Kenya with Ernest Hemingway. Another, with an uncertain grip on history, said he had been on several safaris with Frederick Courtenay Selous. Need I say all the volunteers were big game chancers from way back and looked to me more like big game hunters from Central Park, so all I could do was to make certain they knew one end of a buffalo or a kudu from another and could shoot straight. With the high-speed bullet this was probably more important than anything else. The last thing I wanted to do was wound the animals, because there would be big problems involved in following them up.

At long last we were ready. We looked like a maharajah's *shikar* about to set forth into the uttermost jungles of Uttar Pradesh; all we were short of were a few tambourines, some trumpets and a host of running spearmen. One sergeant with no feeling for the occasion had a PRC10 strapped to his back. Tsk! Tsk! The rest of the column crowded round us, intrigued, encouraging us on with word and gesture, not all of them polite.

On a word of command from Kitale the elephants knelt down. This was a historic moment. I seized it.

'Safari party – prepare to mount – mount!'

The romantic words of command took me back to my days when I commanded a troop of armoured fighting vehicles in C Squadron 2 Reconnaissance Regiment in the Far East.

The safari party mounted awkwardly, two men to each beast. Another word of command from Kitale and the elephants stood up. One of my idiots let me down badly by ending up facing the wrong way round. What can you do with them? Two of the new mahouts fell off amidst much laughter from the crowd, so we had to go through the kneeling down, standing up drill again. Finally Kitale gave the order to advance and we lumbered slowly down to the river's edge. Tarzan calls followed us all the way.

Kitale and I led the column on our beautiful horses, riding side by side. It was a proud moment. I felt like that single horseman who comes dashing into the Spanish bullring and acknowledges the cheers of the crowd with a bow and a wave of his hat. Hans was more or less alongside, mounted on the leading elephant, a magnificent beast but not looking too happy.

'That one in the front is called Ndoromo,' said Kitale. 'He's been here at the Garamba for over thirty years. He's the leader.'

We stopped at the river's edge. Kitale spoke softly to Ndoromo and urged him forward. The elephant slithered down the bank, launched himself onto the water like a small barge and swam the seventy metres to the opposite side slowly and ponderously. The other elephants followed him, trunk to tail, one after another in a perfect drill formation. The column emerged from the other bank, glistening wet, the men marvelling at their new-found prowess as elephant drivers. The intelligent beasts broke into a fast walk straight down the sandy white track.

'Can you really talk to them?' I asked Kitale. 'Can they really understand you?'

'Of course they can. Look.'

We caught up with Ndoromo. Kitale said '*Arrêtez*' quietly, and Ndoromo halted. '*Avancez*,' and we were off again. Tone of voice was more important than the words you used, he said. Words of command they could learn through training, but elephants understood tone instinctively.

If I had been better able to communicate in Swahili and French with Kitale, who was a highly intelligent man and extremely capable, I would have told him the story about the elephant in Dublin zoo which had fallen sick shortly after its arrival from India. He would have appreciated it better than anybody. The new arrival had refused to eat and its strength was fading fast. Soon it went into a decline from which it seemed nothing could rescue it. For all the veterinarian skill brought to bear, there was no obvious cause for its illness. The authorities were baffled. One day Rudyard Kipling, the famous author, who was living in Dublin at the time, hearing of their dilemma asked the superintendent of the Phoenix Park Zoo if he might visit the sick elephant privately. He did. Every day for two weeks he just stood quietly next to the giant animal and spoke to it in Hindustani, in a loving tone. After a week the elephant began to pick up, began to eat once more and eventually recovered. It had been homesick for its Indian mahout and the sound of his voice speaking Urdu. Every schoolboy on his first day back at boarding school will know how it felt, I am sure.

We covered about ten kilometres in the first hour. The view from horseback was excellent and from an elephant's back it must have been better still. Kitale halted the column and pointed into the bush on our right. A few hundred metres off the track was a waterhole. An enormous herd of buffalo, maybe three or four hundred strong, were standing on the far side, shoulder to shoulder, their horns clicking. We approached steadily. Now that the buffalo could see us, they inspected us with seeming venom. A leading bull began to paw the ground, lowered his head and backed off into the herd. They didn't look so tame to me. Kitale gave me the signal. We could select targets and fire when we were ready.

I had anticipated the moment, debating within myself the established ethics which govern big game hunting from elephants. To hunt and kill a wild animal from a motor vehicle, for instance, is regarded as reprehensible behaviour. What then were the Queensbury Rules in these circumstances? Was the hunter permitted, by *shikari* custom, to fire from the back of an elephant? If he was, what about practical considerations? How would an elephant react to the crash of gunfire so close to its ear? I never gave myself time to work that one out. Suddenly I saw very clearly that the angle of declination would make it extremely difficult, if not impossible, for my elite corps of first-time hunters to kill an animal from this height, not to mention the problem of taking a good aim from such an insecure firing position. Accordingly I asked Kitale to lower the men to the ground floor, where they would stand a better chance. Kitale gave the words of command and the elephants knelt obediently.

We shot three buffalo. It was a bit like murder. The animals must have spent the last few years trusting everybody who came to the park, and have known no reason to fear man. But now! It was a tragic betrayal! The rest of the herd galloped off into the surrounding bush in panic. But after a few minutes everything was still once more and the white egrets settled on their branches again. We pushed on, deep into the bush, following up the herd. And so the day wore on. By three in the afternoon we had shot enough animals for our present needs. Now it was a question of getting the carcases back to our camp, the other side of the Dungu river. The mahouts dismounted and followed Kitale to a shed which contained some wooden sleds and two flat-backed trek carts. Whenever we came to an animal we had killed earlier, Kitale would speak to Ndoromo, who communicated in some manner with his brother elephants. They lifted the buffalos or kudu between them and placed them on the sled which they then towed back to the track. From there they hoisted the dead animals onto the backs of the trek carts. My men pushed these laboriously down the sand track in front of them, groaning and moaning every step of the way. It was quite heavy going.

I wondered how we would manage when we got to the river. As it turned out, it was a sight I shall remember for the rest of my days.

The trek carts stopped at the edge of the bank. The men dragged the buffalo and kudu carcases off the carts and piled them side by side on the ground. Kitale ordered Ndoromo to get the dead animals over to the other side of the river. The giant pachyderm sized up one of the buffaloes carefully, took a good grip of its tail with its trunk and dragged it slowly down the slippery bank into the water. Then it towed the carcase across, dragged the buffalo up onto the flat bank, left it there and swam back again. The other elephants did the same. In under an hour all the dead animals were laid out in a row in front of the warden's hut. It was a magnificent performance.

Now it was evening and the sun was sinking fast. A peacefulness had settled on the bush. It was the magic moment when nature signals to the animal kingdom that day is done. Insects ceased to drone, obediently. Birds disappeared from view. The sky began to turn imperceptibly darker, from azure finally to dark blue, so that now it glowed like some precious sapphire. A solitary star, Venus probably, twinkled vigorously, close to the setting sun.

It was a fabulous moment. I determined to capture it on film for posterity. I sent for Hans. He clicked his heels and bowed briefly from the waist.

'*Herr Oberst Leutnant,*' I began, 'kindly let me have the

camera I lent you for one day three weeks ago and which you have neglected to return. Hasten, my bold Hessian, before the light fails.'

Hans clutched his ample stomach and went pale. I wondered if he had been unable to restrain himself and had eaten some buffalo steak, raw. He decided to make a clean breast of it.

'*Herr Kolonel. Mea culpa.* I've lorst it.' He got the pronunciation from Major Wicks, who had been to Harrow.

I didn't know whether to have him tied to a tree and smeared with honey or to bury him in sand up to his neck in the elephant stockade. As neither seemed severe enough, I let him go.

But that's why no photograph of that momentous occasion exists.

Anybody wishing to visit the Garamba National Park today would be advised to write to the Commissariat Général du Tourisme, Kinshasa, Zaïre, in the first place. It is of course very much more sophisticated and well appointed than it was when we visited it in the middle of a rebellion. The park now has an airstrip for tourist aircraft and I would imagine is open to wheeled traffic also. Nagero camp has six bungalows with two beds in each, showers, electricity, a restaurant and bar. The main camp at Gangala-Na-Bodio has two bungalows, two rooms in each, with showers, a restaurant and bar, but oil lamps instead of electricity. It is one of the last refuges on the continent for white rhino and has thousands of elephants, a few of them trained, and a multiplicity of all types of game, including many species of giraffe. I don't know for certain but I imagine that big guy Ndoromo is still there.

13
A Warrior for the Working Day

Dungu was on our general line of advance from Faradje to Niangara. It was an uninteresting town as towns went in the Oriental province of the Congo, but it was unique in one respect. It boasted a castle. A real castle, not a modern, suburban excrescence but the genuine thing.

It was entirely authentic in concept and execution. It had a drawbridge, a moat, a keep and machicolations. In case you are wondering what those last things are, I shall give you the benefit of my dictionary, which I also had to consult. They are the openings between the corbels through which combustibles, molten lead, stones etc could be dropped on the heads of over-enthusiastic assailants. And of course the castle came complete with watchtowers, loopholes, rampart walks, crenels and merlons; you can look the last two up for yourself. But take my word for it, if you had stumbled upon this pile unawares, you would have sworn you were back in the days of Camelot and Richard Harris. It was the sort of place King Hamlet's ghost would have been quite happy to haunt.

The accommodation was generous and amounted to some forty rooms, most of them overlooking the Dungu river, but none of them, at the time of our occupation, equipped with running hot or cold chambermaids, or anything else for that matter. The main hall was spacious but bare. Some animal skins had been spread over the uneven flagstones, others were stretched upon the walls. Several heavy refectory tables strewn with pewter tankards, on chains, provided an authentic touch. All that was needed to make the step back in time totally convincing were a few lazy Irish wolfhounds, salivating at the mouth, to keep the serfs at bay.

But at this moment the serfs were members of 52 and 54 Commandos. The varlets were resting. Our main contact with the enemy was further on at Niangara, and in a day or so these two units would have to sally forth and subdue the enemy. The temporary chatelain was that dour character Lieutenant Joe Wepener. He filled the role with a proprietary air, an enormous bunch of iron keys suspended from his belt. Once a day he would visit the dungeons, dank underground cells, damp and mildewy, in which he had incarcerated a few of his bad lads.

Joe had researched the castle's origins and discovered that it had been built in the early days of the Belgian Congo by an eccentric Belgian administrator named Schollaert, perhaps, as rumoured, with the misuse of public funds and local labour. However, here it was and, from the look of it, I would say it was here to stay, a permanent fixed asset, and possibly one which could be converted by a daring entrepreneur, in time to come, into an hotel. Its situation, conveniently close to the Garamba National Park at Gangala-Na-Bodio, prompted the suggestion.

But this day the baronial hall was crowded with off-duty soldiery, the majority of them drinking from litre bottles of Simba beer in a refined manner, inasfar as such a thing is feasible. There was a hushed air of expectancy about the gathering brought to a sudden climax by Joe in less than one minute flat. After two or three loud smacks on the table with his cane, all conversation ceased.

'Now pay attention, you lot. We are gathered here today to pay our last respects to Volunteer Jim Corbett who was killed in action when we took Aba some weeks ago. In keeping with 5 Commando custom we are auctioning Jim's belongings for the benefit of his dependents. In this case his only dependent is his daughter, Colleen, a little girl of seven.' He held up a snapshot. Those in front could see a shy party in a frilly dress with a pink bow and patent leather shoes. Joe continued. 'This little girl is all alone in the world now. Her mother ran off some time ago, I am told, and Jim's cousin is looking after her for the time being. We understand she will have to go into some sort of institution quite soon, sorry to say. In due course Colleen will get the indemnity for her father's death, and this will be held in trust for her by lawyers until she is twenty-one. In the meantime she will need a bit of help. That's where we come in. Got the picture? Now stand up.'

Joe intoned a short prayer in which Jim's name was mentioned and in this manner our last respects were deemed to be paid. The men sat down again.

The auctioneer was then brought in and introduced formally, which was quite unnecesary, as everybody knew him already as Sergeant Sammy Shoesmith, the intelligence sergeant and assistant to Lieutenant Hans Germani, the IO. He took his stand behind the table amid much hand-clapping and mock cheering. Despite his alleged occupation in the unit, he had, in fact, worked in the distant past as a proper auctioneer in his native Yonkers. He had just come back, rather earlier than expected, from sick leave in the US. It was matter for ribald comment that he had made a remarkably swift recovery from wounds sustained when he was run down by a Congolese ration truck in Aba a few weeks earlier. Rumour had it that this early return to the fold had something to do with the sudden appearance of a jealous Greek husband. Armed. With, apparently, a surprising turn of speed. Or so it was said.

'Well, OK then,' he began, 'I think you guys know what it's all about. I'm going to turn out Jim's kitbag on this table, after which I will auction his possessions piece by piece. Terms of sale: spot cash only. No banana money. None of that stuff from Aba. Only one currency acceptable – genuine greenbacks from the US of A. In small notes only. No hundreds. You know the drill: once the hammer drops, the sale is concluded, then you pay and take the stuff away immediately. I don't want no arguments.' Sammy was a professional.

The kitbag was turned out and a pitiful collection of the dead man's belongings spread themselves out over the table. His washing kit, mess tin, eating-irons, clothes, a Bible without a cover, a mouth organ, a hunting knife, a rosary and a small ivory carving of a Congolese girl's head mounted on an ebony plinth. Jim had probably intended it as a present for his daughter. It was the sort of thing that could have been bought in Bunia for five or six dollars. And an oblong cardboard box wrapped in his spare jump-jacket and trousers and tied with a pullthrough.

Sergeant Shoesmith began at once. Every item was bid up

to seven or eight times its normal value. The dead man had been popular, and this was just about the only way his mates had of showing their feelings for him. The ivory head went for exactly $45. This left the oblong box. Sammy removed its wrappings, opened it up and held the contents above his head for everyone to see. An appreciative murmur circulated rapidly among the many headed.

'Not only is this an exceptional piece of merchandise, my friends, but it is also the rarest commodity in the whole of Oriental province at this very moment. Because of its un-availability I expect it to fetch at least twenty times its intrinsic value.'

Sammy held it aloft with piety as though it were some golden chalice. It was a bottle of Johnny Walker Scotch whisky. A Black Label across one of its square faces pro-claimed its ancient lineage.

'This is not just merchandise, gennelmen, this is liquid gold, the stuff that dreams are made of ... on ... of.' (Sammy had a slight aquaintance with the bard and liked to be accu-rate with his quotations. He also had the makings of a great ham actor.) 'Drink this and all your troubles and fears will vanish. What good is money to you in this god-forsaken part of the world anyway? Tell me that! Tomorrow you may be killed in battle, with your horrible, hard-earned bucks still in your grubby little pockets. Lot of good it will do you then! Now I'm giving you a chance to convert your dollars into instant joy. And remember, it's all in a good cause. Who'll start me off at $100? One hundred I'm bid ... thank you, sir ... who'll give me 110?' He ran on and on, whipping up enthusiasm as he went.

The bidding was brisk but began to wilt at about $190, a little more than a bottle of whisky had fetched at Dramba a couple of months back. For an item which had cost less than $5 at the duty-free shop at Heathrow airport a few weeks earlier it was defying the laws of gravity with a vengeance. Finally it was knocked down to CSM Davy Sandeman for $230 US, almost a month's wages. The sergeant major carried it off in triumph, happy with his purchase. Those who thought he would crack it open there and then were doomed to disappointment.

I arrived at that moment from my headquarters in Faradje. I congratulated the sergeant major on his generosity and mentioned that I was surprised he should have bought the whisky, knowing, as I did, that he was a strict teetotaller. He said he had bought it for an exceptional purpose. When I asked if he could tell me what that might be, all he would say was that he intended it to be drunk on a very special occasion.

CSM Sandeman was not popular with the men. He never sought their approval at any time. He didn't need to. He believed in rigid discipline. He had never known anything else all his life. He was not a sadist, he was perfectly normal in all things, but there was no milk of human kindness in him whatsoever. This was not surprising when you knew his background. His father, a regular soldier, had been killed on the North-West Frontier in 1937, when Davy was only four or five years old. His mother had died in a German air raid on the East End of London in September 1940, leaving him an orphan. He went to school at the Duke of York's Royal Military School at Dover and at the age of fifteen began his boy service with the Gloucesters. Later, as a corporal, in Korea, he took part in the heroic action which earned his famous regiment fresh battle honours and worldwide acclaim. In 1960 he emigrated to Rhodesia and joined the Rhodesian Army, finding his way after a while into the elite SAS company. Soldiering and action were synonymous for him. Barrack-room soldiering was merely a temporary existence which he was not prepared to tolerate as a permanent way of life.

Sandeman's unit was moving up to Niangara the next day. 52 and 54 Commandos had been ordered to seize the bridge, expel the enemy and open up the town again to the thousands of Congolese villagers who had been living in the nearby bush, too scared of the rebels to return to their homes. But on their arrival at Niangara the unit found to their astonishment that the town was deserted. The enemy had already withdrawn into the bush. Lieutenant Wepener put the town into a state of defence and awaited events.

A day or two later the Simbas attacked in vast numbers. They swarmed across the bridge in their thousands and advanced on 54 Commando's dug-in positions from a flank, screaming their war-cry 'Simba! Simba! Mayi! Mayi! Lumumba!' It was touch and go for 54 Commando as the battle ebbed and flowed down the narrow streets and into the town square, forcing Joe's men to abandon their carefully sited positions and fall back on the reserve ones. Joe believed in defence in depth, which was just as well. Now came the huge mob of hyped-up rebel soldiers, waving palm leaves in front of them in the belief that this would give them protection from bullets. Over 5,000 of them advanced in line abreast, in a solid phalanx, across the town square.

On the opposite side CSM Sandeman sat quietly behind a Vickers machine-gun and waited. He was alone. His gun crew lay on either side of him, dead. Calmly he checked the gun, the tripod, the breech cover, the belt, the alignment of the ammuniton boxes, the condenser can. Everything was just as it should be. He tugged at the belt. It would feed perfectly. He was a perfectionist; this was his beloved profession. He flattened the back sight. His fingers curled round the wooden grips, his thumbs resting lightly on the firing button. In his mind's eye he could see the illustration for 'the correct firing position' in the *Manual of Small Arms Training, Vickers MMG, Part 1*. He smiled to himself. Strange to think of that now. On came the Simbas in short forward rushes, screaming and yelling, an avalanche of humanity, surging towards him like waves on the sea shore. Bullets began to hit the wall high above him, showering him with plaster. Davy held his fire. If it was going to be his last action, he would make sure it was done according to the book.

When the Simbas were less than one hundred metres away he opened fire, in long bursts, traversing slowly from left to right and back again. The front ranks dropped, those behind clambering over the dead and wounded. On they came. Fifty metres. The screams were deafening. Now he fired without stopping. New belt. And began again. Thirty metres. They were almost on top of him. He pressed the firing plate down until his thumbs began to bleed. Steam rose from the can. Then it was all over. A grenade lobbed into his weapon pit killed him outright.

Things now looked desperate for 54 Commando, but the reserve unit, 52 Commando, was brought in from the other side of town at the double, and restored the position. The rebels withdrew, leaving their dead piled up behind them.

Three weeks later I was at Dungu again. It was the scene

exactly as before. Sergeant Sammy Shoesmith had just begun to auction the kits of the five men killed in the action at Niangara. One of them belonged to CSM Davy Sandeman. I wondered whether the bottle of Johnny Walker would be among his effects and what it would fetch this time. But it wasn't. Davy had left a note saying that in the event of his death in action he would like the whisky to be drunk by the six men who would carry his body to the grave. A special occasion indeed. They had done that, passing the bottle from hand to hand, sitting by the freshly filled grave, under the big tree, overlooking the river at Niangara. Then they had flung the empty bottle into the water with a plop and said a thank-you to Davy.

Among his effects was Captain Liddell Hart's *History of the First World War*. It was knocked down to me. I still have it. Inside the cover Sergeant Major Davy had copied out those immortal lines from 'Into Battle' by Julian Grenfell:

> The fighting man shall from the sun
> Take warmth, and life from the glowing earth;
> And find, when fighting shall be done,
> Great rest, and fullness after dearth.

How Davy knew he was going to be killed in that particular action has always puzzled me. But I'm sure he knew.

14

Bula Matari

I had just been received by President Mobutu at his palace at Léo Deux, which was quite close to army headquarters. The audience had been pleasant, and the general was in an expansive mood. He had suggested a short walk in the grounds before we said goodbye.

The palace was built on the edge of a cliff overlooking the Congo river, about eight kilometres from the modern city of Léopoldville. Far below we could see the mighty river surging along in a tumult, brown and muddy, over two kilometres wide, carrying thousands of tons of floating vegetation, papyrus, reeds, sometimes whole islands, down to the Atlantic Ocean at a furious pace. The steady, unvarying movement exerted a hypnotic influence on one's mind, dulling the perception. It was hard to drag your eyes away. I remembered the old Congolese saying, 'If you look at the river long enough one day you will see your enemy floating by'.

We came to a small formal garden on the edge of the cliff. In the middle of some ornamental paving stood a bronze life-sized statue on a massive granite boulder. It showed a short, stocky man in an attitude of unconquerable defiance. He was dressed in the fashion of African explorers of the 1870s and wore a peaked cap. From the back of it hung a short piece of cloth to protect the nape of his neck from the fierce Congo sun.

'Bula Matari,' said the general. 'That's what they used to call him. The breaker of rocks. A hard man.'

It was indeed Henry Morton Stanley, the great explorer. One hand was raised over his eyebrows, shielding his eyes from the sun. Now he gazed everlastingly up the Congo river, as though peering deeply into the uncharted hinterland. No doubt he was thinking of the gruelling three years it had taken him to bring his column from Bagamoyo on the east coast of Africa to where we now stood, Kinshasa, the ancient capital of the Lower Congo. And the hard, interminable grind through steaming jungles and along fast-flowing rivers. The journey had cost him the lives of hundreds of his porters through battle, sickness and disease, and the death of all three of his white officers. Finally he arrived at Kinshasa, with a column reduced to 115 men, women and children.

From the account he has left us of this amazing journey we know that Stanley had to impose the severest discipline on all members of his expedition. Without it he would never have succeeded. Discipline, based no doubt on fear, gave his men a sense of unity and purpose as they hacked their way day after day, month after month, year after year across the unexplored continent. Without discipline the expedition would have ground to a halt and disintegrated months before it had even reached the point where the main Congo river really begins, which we now call Stanleyville. It was a triumph of one man's indomitable spirit over the minds of the men he led and the malignant forces of nature.

The general must have been thinking the same thoughts. 'You know what the Belgians call this statue, don't you?' he asked. I said I didn't. 'They call it *jusque là!*'

Jusque là. Up to there. That seemed a strange name for a statue.

'*Pourquoi, mon général?*'

'Well,' he explained with a smile, 'you must remember that Stanley had marched over 5,000 kilometres in three long years to reach this spot. During that time he had had thousands of Africans from dozens of different tribes under his command. You can imagine what sort of a job that was. You see how he is holding his hand up to his forehead? You think he's shielding his eyes from the sun, don't you? Well, he isn't. Actually he's saying to himself, 'I've had those damn porters *jusque là!* '

15
Congo Coetzee

I had not been long in South Africa before I observed an interesting similarity between the rural Afrikaaner and the rural Irish. Both are built on a generous scale, both are inclined to be raw boned and sometimes, though not as often as popularly imagined, slow of thought and speech. Both types tend to be the butt of jokes making them out to be dim witted, if not completely stupid. Van der Merwe on the one hand and Paddy on the other. Both are basically honest, humorous and fun-loving. Both races produce good soldiers. In his background the Irishman has the Roman Catholic religion as his sheet anchor; the Afrikaaner has the Dutch Reformed Church, with its rigid Calvinistic doctrine, as his. Both practise their religion.

While I had only a handful of Irishmen in 5 Commando, there was quite a large number of Afrikaaners. One of them was a man named Coetzee, Johannes Myburgh Coetzee. He had just turned nineteen, stood six foot four and weighed 220 pounds. He was a superb physical specimen, as most of his compatriots are. I think it must have something to do with the sunshine and the open air and all those mealies they ea' I had asked to see him because I had noticed on his enrolment form that in answer to the question 'Occupation?' he had written 'Film Star.'

When I met him in my office he conceded that 'film star' was perhaps an exaggeration, or a bad translation of the Afrikaans for film actor. But in fact he had appeared in a few movies as a film extra and even had a small part as a stand-in for the leading man in a film about boxing. So he was also a boxer? Oh yes, that was his great love, and in fact he had recently won the Transvaal amateur heavyweight title for his

116

boxing club in Krugersdorp. A few months ago he had turned professional and had engaged a manager who was grooming him for bigger and better things. Like the world title? He laughed. You never know, he said.

But so far the rough side of that life had made little mark on him, no broken nose, no cauliflower ears; although you could say there was a certain slowness about some of his answers. I did quite a lot of boxing in my youth and as a result of it, and general observation, I am convinced that anybody over the age of seventeen runs the risk of permanent brain damage as a result of blows to the head in the boxing ring. Nothing is sadder than to talk to an otherwise fine physical specimen whose thought processes are painfully slow and rambling because of the heavy punishment he may have taken to the head. To be punch drunk is an irreversible condition.

Coetzee was none of those things and was well aware of the dangers. I asked him if he could teach the art of self-defence to some of the other men as part of our physical training programme. He was enthusiastic. So I put him in charge of boxing and left him to liaise with the RSM.

He ran things well. Mercenary soldiers are essentially physical, and they enjoy the rough and tumble of sparring, particularly when they are being taught the art by a pro. I had some photographs taken of Coetzee in our gymnasium which he sent back to his club to show that life at Kamina was not so bad after all.

As a soldier Coetzee was about average, kept himself and his equipment clean and was brave. Furthermore he understood and accepted the necessity for strict discipline. Apparently he was an orphan and had been brought up in an institution, so army life was no great hardship or anything particularly unusual for him. He was one of the Stanleyville column and came through that gruelling ordeal without a scratch or a blemish to show for it.

In the meantime I had got to know him very well. Although I never discussed these things with him, I fancied he would never succeed in the ring to any marked degree. I felt he was too emotional for the professional ring, too mercurial of temperament, not stolid enough in his outlook. Added to which he was a thinking animal and unusually introverted for such a physical type. The other side of him was a little strange too, given his background. He was a committed Christian and one of the few men I have ever met in my life who had the moral courage to kneel by his bed in a barrack room and say his prayers in front of the other men. Of course it would have been a foolhardy man who would have tried to make fun of him, so he had that going for him too.

At the end of the first contract he told me he'd had enough and returned to Krugersdorp with my best wishes and thanks for his loyal service. I never gave him another thought after that.

The years passed. I travelled all over the world, spent three years in the Mediterranean on a sailing ship, worked in the Far East, got myself involved in a little skulduggery here and there and eventually returned to South Africa once more, where I bought the Old Vicarage in Hilton, an English-type village in Natal, not far from the capital, Pietermaritzburg, and more or less settled down.

An opportunity was offered to me in 1980 and 1981 to organize and lead a *coup* against the Marxist government of the Seychelles islands, which I accepted. The *coup* proved abortive and although it had been supported, armed and to a large extent financed by the South African Government, they abandoned me when things went wrong. In the ensuing trial they left me to fend for myself. 'Put not your trust in princes, nor in any child of man: for there is no help in them'. You can say that again! In the South African Supreme Court of Justice I was sentenced to ten years' imprisonment on each of two counts for the so-called hi-jacking of an Air India Boeing 707, in which I had brought the men back from Mahé to Durban, despite the fact that this was done at the suggestion and with the full co-operation of the pilot. (That story is told in my book *The Seychelles Affair*.)

So in due course I found myself in Pretoria Central Jail doing time as a hard-labour criminal along with about one thousand others. The chances of mixing freely with the other prisoners were negligible and severely limited to those in one's own cell block. So I was pleasantly surprised one day to get a message, via a friendly warder, from a prisoner named Coetzee, who just wanted to say hullo. As that name is as common as Smith or Robinson elsewhere, it didn't mean much to me. It was a nice thought anyway. But the warder wanted to make sure I had got the message.

'Don't you know him?' he asked.

'Coetzee? Maybe. What's his first name?'

'I don't know, but we call him Congo. Congo Coetzee. Surely you must remember him? He tells us he was in the Stanleyville column with you. Says he was your bodyguard and saved your life on one occasion.'

'Oh yes! That Coetzee. That's right, he did. At Kindu. Shot a rebel who was just about to fire on me. Well I'm damned! What the hell's he doing here? Please tell him I'd like to see him again if that's possible.'

It wasn't. But three months later Congo Coetzee and I met at the prison hospital quite by chance. He hadn't changed much, filled out a lot of course and seemed, if anything, a little bit slower on the uptake.

'What happened, Congo?'

'Manslaughter,' he said. 'Bar fight. Another bloke was giving me a hard time and I told him to watch it, eh. That ended up in a right ding-dong. Man, how was I to know he had a ruptured spleen? Died two days later. Magistrate said as I was a professional boxer I should have known better, and the public must be protected against people like me. Gave me the coat, twelve to fourteen. Only got five more to go.'

We handed each other our cards. This was the accepted etiquette in prison. The identity card recorded one's offence and sentence.

'Remission?'

'Oh yes. Of course. I've been a good *ou*. Should get at least a third off. They tell me I can expect to get out in two years' time.'

'So how've you been?'

'OK. Yourself?'

'OK. Get any visits?'

'No. Haven't had a visit in seven years. Don't want one now. Who's going to visit me anyway? I've got no relations, remember? Don't know a soul on the outside. But I'm not worried. They tell me things are different.'

'Sure are. How are you for groceries?'

We could buy $7 worth of groceries once a month if we had the money.

'Not too bad. I'm in the carpenters' shop. I'm on $2 a

month gratuity. Not much, man, but it's better than nothing.'

He hadn't really altered with the years. Still the same self-sufficient character, no trace of self-pity. A real man.

'Well, nice seeing you, Congo. Keep in touch.'

'Bye, Colonel.'

And our ways parted again, this time for nearly two years. But something terrible happened on the way. The awful story came to me in an unexpected manner from an unimpeachable source, as they say in prison circles.

I was doing my hard labour in the hospital now, scrubbing floors, making tea for the warders, serving grub to the patients at meal times. Pretty soft sort of hard labour you could say, but boring as hell. Meanwhile I had become friendly with one of the hospital prison officers, a highly intelligent and humane man. We'll call him Christiaan. He was of course an Afrikaaner, as indeed was the entire Prison Services staff. One day just after the first count he sent for me.

'Close the door, Mike,' he said. 'Lock it. I don't want to be disturbed. Do you know a man named Coetzee? Congo Coetzee?'

'Yes, sir. He was one of my men in the Congo. Why?'

'He tried to kill himself last night. I'm going to tell you what I think happened. I want you to tell me if I'm right.'

The extraordinary story came out bit by bit. Congo Coetzee, who was now a full blooded man of about thirty-six, was going slowly mad with sexual frustration. Any relief which he could have obtained from masturbation had long since ceased to be an option. In any case his religious beliefs rebelled against the misuse of his body, something in which he had always taken a great pride. He had been brought up to believe it was God's temple, and he did believe it. But in time he had begun to mix with the effeminate types who are present in gaol more or less in the same proportion as they are outside. Inevitably, as with very many long-termers, he experimented with sodomy. His moral reaction to this disgusting practice almost drove him insane. He sought the advice and support of the prison chaplain, who counselled him wisely, had him moved to a different part of the prison and for a time saved him from himself. But it happened again. And again. In a flood of remorse he resolved to punish himself so that he would never be able to sin in this manner again.

That morning at five o'clock they sent for Christiaan urgently. When they unlocked his cell they found Congo lying naked on the floor, covered with blood, his legs wide apart. He had castrated himself with a razor blade.

'Bloody hell!' I said, shocked. 'Will he live?'

'Oh yes. Of course.' Christiaan had seen it all, many times before. Bungled attempts at suicide were not uncommon. Some were bungled deliberately just to gain sympathy. Very few succeeded. 'We'll get him right, but what's going to happen to his mind? That's what I'd like to know.'

We discussed the cause of the tragedy. Christiaan wanted to know if I thought Congo was deranged before the attempt. I said I didn't know but I doubted it. He may not have been very bright, was probably a bit punchy too, but he knew right from wrong and had decent moral values.

Christiaan said he would get him transferred to Zonderwater Prison as soon as he recovered. A new environment might help him take a new look at life.

'Do you think they'll regard it as attempted suicide?' I asked.

'Yes. Could be.'

'Will it affect his parole?'

'It might. They'll have to take it into account anyway.'

As I never heard any more about Congo Coetzee, I assumed he had recovered and gone to Zonderwater. I hoped so. I knew he was popular with the prison staff, so he stood every chance of getting a maximum remission of sentence if he continued to behave well. Many of the prison officers knew him intimately and quite a few of them had gained rapid promotion during the seven or eight years he had already served. Some of them were generals in the service by now.

Now I was working as a plumber's mate on a new prison we were building two kilometres away from Pretoria Central. We marched there and back every day. It was a better life than being cooped up all day like an animal, and I tried to teach myself the trade, which I found interesting. About eleven o'clock one morning my warder sent for me. He was an Austrian immigrant, a disciplinarian who did everything according to the book. But he was fair, knew his job as a qualified plumber himself and was one of the few who was prepared to teach the black prisoners whenever he had the time, which wasn't very often. I liked him.

'Visit, Mike,' he announced, flatly.

A visit at eleven in the morning of a working day was unheard-of. Visits were allowed only on a Saturday or Sunday, one every three or four weeks, and lasted forty minutes.

'You sure it's for me, sir?'

'Of course. Get changed and I'll take you down in ten minutes. Somebody wants to see you at the officers' *menasie*. I've been told to take you to the generals' mess. Thirty minutes only.'

'Is it a general, then?'

'I don't know. And I wouldn't tell you if I did. Be quick. Can't hang around all day.'

He delivered me to the ante-room of the officers' mess and waited outside the door. I went in. It was empty. I stood for a while inhaling the smell of furniture polish and lino, examining the potted plants, sports trophies and photographs of rugby fifteens and cricket elevens which adorned the walls. After a minute or two a man in his middle thirties came in. He was clean-shaven and very strongly built. He was wearing a light cream suit. He looked like a successful life-assurance salesman.

'Hullo, Colonel. Don't you remember me?'

I looked closely at him. Blimey O'Reilly! It was Congo Coetzee!

'Good grief! Congo ! So you're out!'

'Got out yesterday. The generals gave me this outfit and have found me a job. I'm travelling in children's clothing – can you believe it? Me! Main line, Jo'burg to Ladysmith.'

I congratulated him. Nothing a prisoner likes better than to see a long-termer get out. He looked great. He was right on top. But when my thirty minutes were up I couldn't help asking him how he'd arranged the visit. It was unbelievable.

'No problem,' he said. 'The generals know me well. We're old mates. I knew some of them when they were senior warders. I just asked them as a special favour if I could see you.'

That puzzled me.

'But why me, Congo?'

He looked down at his feet and examined his fingernails.

'You're the only man in the world I know,' he said, '...and,' he added quietly, 'respect.'

I might have answered him if I wasn't so choked up, but I was saved by the Austrian warder, who came in at that precise moment.

'Come on, Mike. Time's up. Back to work.'

16
A Painful Episode

The cocktail party was being held on the Berea, an elite part of Durban, in the South African province of Natal, generally reckoned to be the last outpost of the British Empire. With some reason. It was an elegant affair: only the very best people had been invited. In a far corner of the fashionable salon a young girl of twelve or thirteen, the daughter of the house, sat at a Steinway grand piano, improving, with some hesitation, on Rubenstein's 'Melody in F'. Red-sashed Indian waiters circulated discreetly among the guests, carrying trays of champagne and tempting morsels to eat. The scene could have been set anywhere in Mayfair, Manhattan or the 16th arrondissement.

Katanga and its troubles were light-years away, but our charming but feather-headed hostess had heard about them ... vaguely. She had also heard about me ... vaguely. Her son had been one of my officers. She took me by the hand and led me deftly to a formidable cluster of elderly ladies who appeared to have taken root in a sofa.

'This is Major Mike Hoare,' she said. 'He's just back from the Katanga, where he's been fighting for Mr Tshombe ... or was it Mr Lumumba?... against the ... er, Baluba, wasn't it? Anyway, he's had the most hair-raising experiences, haven't you, dear Major? Do please tell us all about them!'

The dowagers with one accord raised their lorgnettes and examined me closely. When they were satisfied there was nothing notifiably contagious about my person, one of them, the ringleader I am tempted to say, if dowagers have ringleaders, addressed me in a deep and sonorous voice.

'Do tell me, Major ... what was it like to be caught by the Balubas?'

I was impressed with the pincer-like movement of her hands as she posed the question. To a certain extent it suggested my reply. There was a tangible silence as I searched for the *mot juste*.

'Excruciating!' I said, and fled.

17

To Me Wild Geese!

Once more we were at Albertville on the shores of Lake Tanganyika. It felt like a home-coming. I was beginning to assume proprietary rights over this magnificent stretch of water, 720 kilometres long and fifty to sixty kilometres wide, a veritable inland sea. Its very name seemed to evoke romance, reaching out to me from those wonderful books by Livingstone, Burton, Speke, Grant and Stanley which had been the companions of my boyhood. I had been re-reading Stanley. He and Livingstone had explored the northern end of Lake Tanganyika shortly after their meeting at Ujiji, which was just across the lake from us, twelve kilometres south of present-day Kigoma. But I looked in vain for any reference he might have made to the Ubware peninsula, the narrow neck of land which juts out from the coast 160 kilometres north of Albertville, to enclose Burton Bay. This peninsula was of particular interest to me at this moment.

Livingstone and Stanley had canoed their way up the lake to examine the Ruzizi estuary, and in passing to the east of the Ubware had thought it was an island and not a peninsula. Stanley certainly shows it as such in the map which accompanies his book *How I Found Livingstone*. For them this was of no great consequence, but for me, one hundred years later, the fact was fraught with a potential danger.

A glance at the map shows that the distance between the northern tip of this peninsula and Tanganyika is a bare twenty-five kilometres. Munitions of war were being ferried across the lake from Kigoma to Baraka, a rebel stronghold on the shores of Burton Bay, via this route at a feverish pace. Apart from being a commercial centre of some importance, the town itself also had a religious significance. The word *baraka* is Arabic and is a term used among the Berbers to indicate the quality of holiness of people and things. As the *Encyclopaedia Britannica* says, 'It is inherent in corn, bread, trees, especially palms and olives, wells, springs, stones, rocks, caves, sometimes animals or birds.' Furthermore, *baraka* is extremely sensitive to pollution and can easily be spoilt – for example, by contact with infidels. The word can also describe something akin to faith, good luck, a charmed existence. Accordingly the town held a special place in the minds of its inhabitants, the vast majority of whom followed the Mohammedan faith.

Masses of war *matériel* from Communist sources had been piling up in Kigoma, and much of it was being ferried across the narrow strait to the Ubware by night, in all manner of transports from fast launches to home-made rafts and dug-out canoes. As most of the lake journey took place on the Tanganyika side of the border, the voyage was not a major risk for the rebel forces. It was reckoned by our intelligence sources that the rebels were being supplied in this way by about thirty tons a day. This, together with the influx of Cuban mercenary soldiers under the leadership of Che Guevara, posed a considerable threat to the Congolese government. The task now given to us was to stop this flow of arms and ammunition as speedily as possible.

For this purpose I was given an eighty-ton ship named *Ermans*, six PT boats and about forty men who would form the nucleus of a navy. Regrettably the majority of these men had never set foot in a boat before, but, as I have related in an earlier story, they were soon licked into reasonable shape by Tom Harrison, who was raised to the rank of captain and appointed OC the Navy.

At the beginning of a new contract my routine had been to interview each recruit thoroughly. Experience had taught me that there were many who had volunteered under erroneous impressions – for example, that they were joining the Foreign Legion or that it was going to be a boozer's paradise, or that they could opt for garrison duties, which they thought, wrongly, would entail a minimum risk to their persons etc. I had to disabuse their minds on all of these scores while at the same time trying to find the soldierly material I needed to enable me to do the task laid on the unit by the C-in-C, General Mobutu.

A tall, lean character now stood in front of me. He was about twenty-five, I would say. He handed me a paper which gave his personal particulars. In answer to the question 'Occupation?' he had written 'Poet.' I had another look at him. Yes, I supposed he could be. That would make an interesting change from some of the rougher element the recruiting officers were now sending me. Just lately I had been forced to reject about fifty per cent of them as unfit for service. I read the form.

'Sarsfield?'

'Yes, sor.'

I looked up. Irish, obviously. Especially with a name like that. Blue eyes, very white skin and jet-black hair, plenty of it. And a loose, relaxed, unsoldierly appearance.

'Patrick Sarsfield – of course?'

'Yes, sor. You'll be knowing our history, I've no doubt.'

'Yes. As a matter of fact I do. But do you?'

'Indeed I do.'

'A descendant of the first Earl of Lucan perhaps?'

'Maybe aye. Maybe no.'

'But noble, no doubt?' I asked with a laugh.

'Of course. Aren't we all a nation of kings?'

'Indeed. I see you're a poet. Wilfred Owen, Siegfried Sassoon, Major Macrae. Those names mean anything to you?'

'They do. But I'm not a war poet. I'm more of a lover of nature in the raw.'

Curiouser and curiouser.

'Well, tell me what you've been doing since you left school.'

He had been three years at Cork University, studied Gaelic and majored in the history of Ireland. He had knocked around quite a lot since graduation and confessed that a steady nine-till-five job would have killed him. He was never happier than when he was alone in the open under the sky and stars. His ambition was to crystallize the beauties of nature into the sound of words, which he loved. No, he hadn't written anything memorable just yet, but that would come. I had a feeling it very well could. He said all this with a hint of humour and the mildest of musical brogues. With a little imagination I could hear the Atlantic breakers crashing on the Old Head of Kinsale.

'Are you from Limerick?' I asked. 'Just idle curiosity.'

'No.' He named a village somewhere along the River Lee.
'Is Sarsfield your real name?'
'It might very well be.'
I took that no further. It was not for me to pry into his past
or to question him on his antecedents. These matters were,
traditionally in 5 Commando, nothing to do with me or the
Congolese Army. I didn't pursue them but turned to more
important matters, such as his previous military experience,
if any. He shook his head. He had had no military training
whatsoever. But he had been to sea as a sailor, a deckhand
on a fishing trawler out of Cork.

Why had he volunteered to serve with 5 Commando? It
was my stock question; the answers invariably told me everything. Sarsfield's case was no exception. He had crossed
over from Ireland to Santander on a Basque fishing boat, left
the ship and worked his way south through Spain, teaching
English to the children of the wealthy. A year later he
reached Algeciras and took the ferry to Morocco. He had
joined a caravan of Tuaregs near Sidi Bel Abbes, reached
Tamanrasset safely, left them and made his way by lorry to
Kano, hitch-hiked to Lagos, signed on as an able seaman on
a freighter going to Lobito via Boma, jumped ship at Banana
at the mouth of the Congo and then made his way to
Léopoldville. There he met one of my men in a bar, was
intrigued with the 5 Commando Wild Goose badge on his
shoulder, was introduced to our liaison officer at GHQ and
here he was.

This was a pleasant surprise. Poet aside, Sarsfield was the
genuine thing, a real adventurer. I had estimated that less
than five per cent of my recruits were drawn from this
exclusive class, a dying breed, sad to say. I was delighted to
have him. His lack of previous military experience was no
drawback in my eyes. In many cases in the past I had found
that to be a distinct advantage. The problems of soldiering in
the African bush often called for a new line of thought, the
fresh approach uncluttered by a previous training more suitable for a different terrain. Recent experience had taught me
that traditional methods of training were not always the best
or most suitable for the Congo. In the main the really vital
things I looked for in a recruit were physical fitness and a
keenness to learn.

So I sent Patrick Sarsfield down to Tom as an obvious

recruit for the navy.

Sarsfield proved more than adequate. Tom, who was a bit of an oddball himself, was very pleased with him. He described Sarsfield as a strange man, remarking that he did not mix freely with his shipmates but that did not mean he was stand-offish. Certainly he never joined them in the monumental thrashes they indulged in on their return from long patrols 'at sea'. Not the run-of-the-mill Irishman, you could say. Whether or not he found inspiration for poetry as he sailed over the waters of the mountain-rimmed saucer that was Lake Tanganyika I never discovered. He did his work conscientiously and in due course Tom made him quartermaster on the *Ermans*.

From time to time I would sail with Tom to see how he was handling the interdiction programme. An overnight trip in the direction of Kigoma was the one I liked best. There was always the chance of bumping the enemy in the narrow strait between the tip of the Ubware and the Tanganyika coast. As I normally stood in the deckhouse, this brought me into close contact with Sarsfield, who was usually at the wheel. He was not over-communicative by nature but in the small hours of his watch, when I presumed both our defences were down, we would chat idly and sometimes tell each other snippets about our lives. After about a month I probably knew him as well as anybody else in the unit.

He certainly knew his history, which was his subject, and on one occasion I asked him if he could tell me how the Irish soldiers who had left Ireland at the end of the seventeenth century had come by their name, the Wild Geese. They had named themselves, he said. The story was a stirring one.

After the Siege of Limerick in 1691 the defeated Irish made their weary way down the Shannon and down the Lee in their thousands to embark for France, never to return to old Ireland. They were under the command of their much-loved leader, his namesake, Patrick Sarsfield, first Earl of Lucan. It was the time of the October moon. Overhead the autumn skies were darkening with the wings of a thousand geese, eager and strident, crying the coming of a desperate winter. The bedraggled soldiers looked up at the skies and took the name. Thereafter they called themselves 'the Wild Geese'. They were the forerunners of generations of Irish soldiers who would serve as mercenary soldiers in the armies of Louis

XIV and later the Habsburgs, rather than submit to a servile existence under the hated Protestant King William of Orange.

On another occasion he told me that one of his forebears had been a member of the original Wild Geese. A story had been passed down in his family from father to son of the way these aliens in a foreign land stood together in time of trouble. Whenever one of them was in serious danger, surrounded perhaps by an enemy, he would yell out at the top of his voice 'To me, Wild Geese!' Then it was the sworn duty and a matter of sacred honour for all his compatriots within earshot to rally to his assistance, at once and without fail. I liked that. Later I learned that he had introduced that concept among the crew of *Ermans*, who, with the passage of time, had come to admire and respect the strange Irishman. Arising out of this the twenty or so members of the ship's company developed a crew spirit which distinguished them from all the other units making up Tom's navy. Henceforth they looked upon themselves as blood brothers.

It was now time to begin the next operation. A successful outcome could mean the end of the two-year Communist-inspired rebellion which sought to overthrow the Congolese government. My plan was a simple one. Baraka, the port in Burton Bay, had been fortified by the enemy and used as the main depot for war *matériel*, arms and ammunition, ferried across from Tanganyika. Fizi, a hilltop town some fifty kilometres inland, was the rebel headquarters in the north of the province. If Baraka could be seized from the lake and Fizi captured a few days later, the rebellion must crumble. This stroke would also render their enclave at Yungu, further down the coast, impotent. The Cubans would be forced to withdraw and once they had gone it was unlikely the rebellion would continue.

This then became my plan. Phase one – the capture of Baraka after an amphibious assault by 5 Commando, assisted by a battalion of Congolese troops. Phase two – the capture of Fizi, to follow immediately.

So in due course, after two months' intensive training, we embarked for the assault. This was to begin with a twenty-four-hour approach up the lake which would bring us off the beaches eight kilometres north of Baraka just before dawn. The men would be landed by PT boats in successive waves, followed by specially prepared barges which would land the armoured vehicles and jeep transport.

I was under no illusions as to the risk involved and the difficulties inherent in this the most difficult of all military operations. However, we were lucky and everything went exactly to plan – except the most important thing of all, the weather. Contrary to expectations, and against all local weather forecasts, that morning brought a Force 10 wind and a storm, unheard-of for that time of the year. Although this made the beach landing from PT boats dangerous, it was by no means impossible. But it did mean the loss of our air cover. Our Cuban air force, flying T28 fighters and B26 light bombers, was grounded at this critical time. A further problem was the existence, or so I was told, of a sun spot which was making communication by radio extremely difficult.

The first assault troops landed unopposed and gained a small foothold. Successive waves followed rapidly for the next hour or so until a sizeable force, including the Ferret armoured cars, had formed a bridgehead. The advance on Baraka could now begin.

We bumped the enemy's positions on the outskirts of the town in pouring rain. It was obvious the place was heavily defended and they intended to put up a fight for it. After a co-ordinated attack we overran the enemy outposts. But not without loss – one of my officers, Lieutenant Columbic, was killed and several men were wounded. The enemy fell back steadily to prepared positions, but by ten in the morning we had gained a secure foothold in the northern part of the town and our patrols were penetrating as far as the beach. The seizure of the beach was my main intention and the most vital part of my plan. Once we had the beach, *Ermans* and the transports could come right into Burton Bay, where there was more than enough water for them to anchor off quite close and to discharge men and *matériel* for transport directly to the beach in the PT boats. The arrival of those stores and reinforcements was the lynch-pin on which the success of the operation would depend.

As soon as my forward elements reported the beach was in their hands, I moved there with my headquarters and gave the signal for the ships to close in as planned. At this point to my astonishment and considerable chagrin a heavy gun opened up on us from the hills overlooking the port. I sent for Captain Hugh van Oppens, the commander of 52 Commando. He was my expert on heavy weapons. We moved to a point from which we could see where the gunfire was coming from.

Hugh trained his glasses on the top of the hill and waited for the next flash. It came. A thunderous roar, then a whirring sound followed immediately as a huge shell passed over our heads. Then two more in fairly quick succession. A splash 200 metres out in the bay behind us told us the enemy were getting our range.

'What do you make of it, Hugh?'

'No doubt about it, sir. 76 mil cannon. Probably two. Maybe three.'

'Range?'

He raised a rangefinder to his eye. It was one of the few bits of decent equipment we had captured from the enemy in the recent past. Soviet origin, like most of the enemy armament, and highly efficient.

'Five thousand five hundred metres, or thereabouts. I'm not absolutely sure of the site. But near enough.'

'What can we hit them with?'

'Nothing, I'm afraid, sir.' That was a disappointment. 'The best I can suggest is to get my 81 mm mortars as close as I can and then let them hear from us. Maximum range with the charges I've got is about 3,000 metres. Shall I give it a go?'

As he said it, another two 76 mm shells screamed through the air and dropped in the bay closer to us. Heartened by this support the enemy in front of us opened up with everything they had in the way of small-arms fire. It was deafening but not dangerous, as ninety per cent of it went far too high. We dug in with enthusiasm. When the barrage subsided, I ordered Hugh to silence the guns on the hill. Until that had been accomplished we were effectively pinned down. Hugh set off. I checked the time and allowed a full hour before he could get within range and come into action. That hour promised to be a miserable one.

The firing died down on both sides but the 76 mm gun continued its deadly fire, dropping the shells within our perimeter with hateful accuracy. A runner brought me a message saying two men had been killed and a number

wounded in our most forward position. The medical orderlies with our doctor, Couve de Murville, set off to see what
they could do. I sent a signal to *Ermans* to stop where they
were, repeat stop, and not to approach the beach until further orders. The transports behind her, filled with troops and
matériel, must wait until the beach was clear of enemy gunfire.

Fifty minutes had passed since Hugh had gone. I longed
to hear the boom of his mortars. The man was an expert and
I had a gut feeling he would succeed. Just as I was beginning
to feel optimistic, my signaller passed me a message from
Ermans to say they were closing with the beach. I couldn't
believe it. Why were they disobeying my last order? Who had
countermanded it? It was madness. This would wreck my
whole plan, but there she was, steaming steadily for the
shore for all the world to see. There could be no doubt about
it, it was a cast-iron certainty, *Ermans* would be hit by the
enemy guns. It was too big a target to miss, and whoever was
in command of the enemy artillery knew what he was doing.

It was now a race against time. *Ermans* was approaching
the beach and the danger zone steadily at about three knots.
Hugh, I reckoned, must be just about ready to blast off. It
was a question of who opened fire first. A minute later I
heard a dull boom followed by a cheer from some of my men.
Hugh had come into action. I trained my glasses on the
mountain top and saw a tiny plume of yellow smoke slowly
develop into a rising cloud. It was Hugh's ranging shot. Two
more broke out on either side of it. He was registering. Then
came his barrage of high-explosive shells. Simultaneously
the enemy 76 mm guns opened up on us again. I swivelled
round to see if *Ermans* would run the gauntlet of the gunfire
and to my horror heard the scream of a shell as it crashed into
her deckhouse, sending up a dense cloud of smoke and
splintered matchwood. A second shell struck the forecastle
companionway, and the ship stopped. Fire broke out.

A loud cheer drew my attention back to the hillside. Hugh
must have scored a direct hit. We heard no more from the 76
mm cannons, but regrettably it was too late – they had done
their deadly work already.

Five days later we had established our beachhead, captured Baraka and the port and advanced on Fizi only to find

it abandoned. That was a disappointment but we had won the day. In essence, the rebel resistance had been decisively broken, their line of communication had been severed and all that remained would be the tedious task of routing out the enemy from his rabbit warren of defended positions in an area the size of Wales. This would take weeks, if not months. But the end of the rebellion was no longer in doubt.

I was urgently required at headquarters in Albertville and flew down in a Bell helicopter, flying at zero feet well out into the lake. After dealing with the official business I drove round to the general hospital to see how the wounded from *Ermans* were coming along. Twelve of the crew had been seriously injured and three were not expected to live. I wondered who they might be.

The hospital was almost identical with those British General Hospitals I had known in my army days in India, with high ceilings, wide stone verandas and spacious corridors. This one was run by nuns from the local convent. I went in to ask the matron for permission to visit my men. She led me slowly up the stairs, the chink of her keys sounding softly beneath her white serge habit. Slow-moving punkahs stirred the air lazily in every ward, diffusing the reek of anaesthetic and polished floors. We came to a small isolation ward. In the centre of it a man lay in a bed, deathly white. One of his legs had been amputated. His face and torso were heavily bandaged and bloody. His jet-black hair lay on the pillow like a medieval crown. I glanced at the matron. The look of infinite sadness on her face told me all I needed to know. Even as I watched him, I could sense the man was dying. Suddenly he stirred and as though acting on some imperative impulse, using up the last of his strength, he raised his head and shouted out as loudly as he could, 'To me, Wild Geese! To me, Wild Geese!'

The scene that followed has been imprinted on my memory for all time. Hardly had the cry sounded when from all sides of the adjoining wards came the men of *Ermans*, some staggering under the pain of their wounds, some dropping to the floor with pain but crawling there just the same, determined to reach their comrade, deaf to the entreaties of the nuns and orderlies who were trying desperately to stop them. Now they crowded round the dying man's bed and told him they were there, held his hands, spoke softly to him, told him they would never leave him, urged him with tears in their eyes not to die. They promised they would stay with him always.

But he died a few minutes later. I didn't need to be told who he was. I knew it instinctively. It was Patrick Sarsfield.

18
Alice Blue Gown

The second contract had expired and it was time for the men to go home. The wounded had been sent to hospitals in Salisbury and Johannesburg long since. Medical boards would be set up to assess the amount of any compensation due to them. The dead would remain for ever, buried close to where they fell. One or two of them would be remembered for a time by a wooden cross while it lasted, which wouldn't be long.

Any man who wanted a certificate of service to say that he had completed his contract with honour could ask for one. A queue had formed up outside the orderly room door for this purpose. All the certificates were the same and I had signed them in blank the night before. The RSM would fill in the names and issue them. It was an impersonal affair.

But one man, Volunteer Francis Ellis, was not satisfied with the formal wording of his certificate. I could hear him in the passage outside my office, complaining to the RSM.

'Don't bloody well simper,' said the RSM, a hornery old character. He loathed queers. 'March in sharpish, stand up straight for once in your life and ask for what you want. Got it?'

I knew Ellis. He was a medical orderly and a damned good one at that. The men called him Alice. He liked that. It was quite true that his wrist was bent, but there was nothing wrong with his personal courage. I had seen him attending to the wounded under fire and admired his coolness on many an occasion. His morals or his persuasion or whatever were his own affair and no business of mine. From a soldiering point of view he was a first-class medic.

He marched in with two left feet and said his piece. In so

many words, all he wanted was a more personal certificate, something, he said, that he could be proud of. He would like to show it to his friends in Hillbrow.

'Wouldn't you? After all, it's not everyone who has doctored the rude and licentious soldiery in action, I mean, is it? Thank you dear, er ... Colonel!'

I looked at the *pro forma* certificate: 'Volunteer Francis Ellis served as a volunteer in 5 Commando, Armée Nationale Congolaise, for six months and discharged his contract with honour.'

'What's wrong with that?' I asked, 'Says it all, doesn't it?'

But he insisted gently, so I tore it up and wrote him a more personal one, which thrilled him. Lovely! Just what he wanted! He was going to frame it and put it on the wall when he got home.

It read: 'Volunteer Ellis served as a medical orderly in 5 Commando, Armée Nationale Congolaise, for six months. He discharged his contract with honour. During this time he brought great comfort to the men.'

19

The Professionals

Eighty-five per cent of the enlisted men in 5 Commando had had a military training of some sort, five per cent were not soldiers at all in the true sense of the word but adventurers, leaving ten per cent who were genuine professional soldiers.

The majority of the men had enlisted for reasons ranging from being out of work at the time to girlfriend trouble, or family upsets of one sort or another. Contrary to popular belief, the seemingly generous rate of pay was not the prime motivation. Very few men came for a second contract, whereas the professionals signed on regularly time after time. As far as they were concerned, that way of life could go on indefinitely. Which was just as well for me because in every contract it was the professional element which held the unit together and it was from their number, in the main, that officers and NCOs were chosen. In this way the professionals gave the unit its distinctive character and its sense of continuity.

Most of the professionals went from volunteer to captain, the highest rank available to them, in the course of three or four contracts. The rank, need I say, was of secondary importance in most cases to the additional pay involved.

In the stories in this book I may have given, unwittingly, the impression that the mercenary soldiers in my unit were all fine fellows selling their military skills on short-term contract to a grateful government and behaving like gentlemen in the process. That is not the entire truth. Certainly the majority of them behaved in a disciplined manner, but this depended largely on how they were commanded and by whom. It is true to say that their behaviour at all times, in action or out of it, depended on the quality of leadership and discipline they were subjected to. Where this was lacking, their behaviour was frequently abominable and, as can be expected, attracted the attention of the press. It goes without saying that a macho individual back in Salisbury or Johannesburg who had been indulging himself in the Congo as a make-believe soldier, usually terrorizing the civilian inhabitants with his non-existent military expertise, would find a ready audience in a pressman more interested in the bizarre than in the dull day-to-day experiences of the average mercenary soldier. Out of these reports grew an astonishing crop of ridiculous stories which a gullible public seemed quite ready to accept as the truth.

Although the professional element made up only a small proportion of our numbers, it would be fairer to judge the true mercenary soldiers by their performance rather than that of the absurd types described above who went under the general title *'les affreux'*, 'the frightful ones'.

The professionals intrigued me. On one occasion I invited three of them to my quarters at Albertville and recorded a question-and-answer session, with their agreement, to clarify in my own mind subjects like motivation and so on which had long puzzled me. Their answers were enlightening, and looking back on them over the years I see no reason to believe that they have changed much since then.

The three men were all professional soldiers. By that I mean they had joined the army after leaving school, had been trained in a regular army (the equivalent of an apprenticeship) and had served with their colours or elsewhere ever since. All three were sergeants in 5 Commando at this time. The first was an ex-member of the French Foreign Legion, a Scot. He was thirty-two, had enlisted at first in the Scots Guards, served his contract with the British Army and then joined the famous Légion Etrangère, not through any romantic notion but because the French Foreign Legion were actively engaged in fighting at that time in Indo-China.

The second had been a corporal in the SAS Company of the Rhodesian Army and had seen action in Korea and at Suez as a paratrooper. The third had been a sergeant in the Royal Marines who had been seconded to the Omani Scouts as a second lieutenant and had served with me in the Katanga three years before. In most cases they spoke with one voice. I have edited the answers to make them readable.

What attracts you to this way of life?

A mercenary unit of soldiers in these days is unique, so you could say it is the opportunity to practise our skills which attracts us rather than the way of life. We feel that it is only in combat that we can use the skills we have acquired over the years. The ambitions of a soldier can be consummated only by action. If it were not so, much of our training would be pointless.

How do you see your immediate future as mercenary soldiers?

When this show is over we will look for other theatres of war where our services could be in demand, probably as technical advisers or in the training of soldiers. That is our way of life, that is what we have been trained to do. In most cases this will involve enlisting under a foreign flag, making us mercenary soldiers by definition.

Are you ashamed to be called a mercenary soldier?

Of course not. There is nothing dishonourable in selling our military skills for money, providing we do an honest day's work for a fair day's wages. We are no more mercenary than a journalist selling his skill to a newspaper or an estate agent selling his expertise to the public in the property market. True there are no considerations of violent action connected with those professions but action is in the very nature of soldiering.

What principles do you think should be employed in the use of mercenary soldiers in Africa?

They should be used only in support of existing national armies, either as fighting men or as technical advisers. They should not be used as members of private armies or to support rebel movements or they will soon be labelled gangsters and bandits.

Have you any politics?

We tend to be anti-Communist as a result of our experiences worldwide but we adhere to the principle that politics should be left strictly to politicians. Soldiers are the men who execute the ultimate decisions of politicans. It complicates things when soldiers start pontificating about politics in the course of their duties. Fortunately at our level it is not something which is likely to bother us much but even so today's mercenary soldier has got to keep abreast of the local political situation if he values his skin. Things change so rapidly in Africa, sometimes overnight!

What do you think of your fellow soldiers of fortune?
Not a lot. Good chaps most of them but inclined to drink too much. Few of them are as dedicated to the job as we would like them to be. The majority of them are amazed that they can get killed or seriously wounded in action! What they thought they were volunteering for we can't imagine.

Would you sell your services to the highest bidder?
You joke, surely! What highest bidder? You sound like a badly informed radio interviewer. You know as well as we do that the formation of this unit as part of the Congolese National Army arose as a result of exceptional political circumstances which are unlikely ever to happen again. The possibility of a counter bid for our services in these circumstances by a foreign power is ludicrous. Who is likely to make such an offer? The idea is absurd. For a start who could afford to make such a bid? Anybody with the slightest acquaintance with the cost of keeping 500 mercenary soldiers in the field in the manner to which they have become accustomed will know it is prohibitive. It is an undertaking which can be accomplished only at government level. It's not for nothing that the United States of America and Belgium are footing the bill for this effort. The assumption is that they think the Congo is worth saving from the Communist threat which nearly overwhelmed it in 1964.

But let us examine a hypothetical question on the assumption that at some time in the future we may be fighting for some other power and out of nowhere comes a counter-offer for our services. Somewhere in South America perhaps. Would we accept? The probabilities are remote in the extreme. We must assume that we accepted the original contract in the first instance because it was satisfactory. If it remained satisfactory and its clauses were being honoured, the assumption is that we would continue to honour it on our side. The known is usually more acceptable than the unknown. We know of no case in recent times in which a mercenary soldier has swopped sides for better terms. Or was even offered them for that matter. The question itself probably has its roots in the Middle Ages when all armies were mercenary armies and counter-bids for their services quite conceivable.

Have you a family of your own?
No. The time will come, I suppose, when we will want to settle down but it won't be for a long time yet. In any case marriage and the raising of a family are not really compatible with this way of life.

What will happen when you are too old to serve in action?
Well, the security business has developed so swiftly in the last few years, we expect we would be in demand for specialist employment of some sort or another. Bodyguards to famous personalities perhaps. Or riding shotgun on a payroll truck!

What do you think of our rates of pay?
Reasonable for soldiers in barracks, but there should be a sharply higher scale for men in action. Danger money as presently paid should be only for those engaged in actual combat. It is unfair that office wallahs should get the same as us just because they are in the area designated by GHQ as a danger zone. That said, the risks we face are out of all proportion to the monetary reward. What money can compensate you for the loss of an eye or an arm?

What improvements could you suggest for the unit?
On the assumption that the unit will continue in being for some years, there should be a proper depot, somewhere like Bunia, for instance, and the unit should be given a fixed establishment as an integral part of the Armée Nationale Congolaise. French and Swahili should be taught. The men should be offered Congolese nationality and a chance to buy land and settle here. And all our pay should be in hard currency and not as at present, half US dollars and half Congolese francs.

Do you see any future for mercenary soldiers in Africa?
No long-term future. Not as a unit anyway. Our present set-up is exceptional and came about only because you persuaded General Mobutu that a composite unit of mercenary soldiers would be more effective in putting down the rebellion than his original plan of spreading them thin, using them as technical advisers to units of the Congolese Army. We think you were right in those special circumstances. But

where a country has a reasonably efficient army, we think mercenary soldiers could be employed more profitably as technical advisers rather than as fighting men. You may remember the US Army sent several hundred advisers in this way to help the Saigon army long before President Kennedy decided to send US troops to Vietnam.

What do you think of the weapons we use?
Adequate. As they are exactly the same as those used by NATO, we can hardly criticize. But we think the calibre of modern automatic rifles is excessive and results in over-kill or, as is probably intended, over-wounding. The Japanese appreciated this during World War II. While we used a .303 bullet, theirs was down to .265, which proved just as effective and of course solved many administrative problems.

Which is better in your opinion, the FN or the AK47?
We think the FAL rifle is superior to the Kalashnikov in its manufacture but there's not much in it. The AK is a typical mass-produced effort, crude but highly effective. But a lot depends on where they were made. The Hungarian ones seem to be superior to the Romanian and Yugoslav examples. Strange that the world has accepted without comment the unbelievable number, millions in fact, of AK47s which have flooded into every country in Africa since World War II, all supplied by the Soviet Union and its satellites. Did they sell them or did they give them away to encourage rebellion, Communist-fashion? We wonder what the western world's reaction would have been had Africa been flooded with, shall we say M16s, Uzi sub-machine-guns or Lee Enfields? Might have raised a few eyebrows, we suppose.

Can you use a Vickers MMG?
Yes, we're happy to say. For sustained fire-power it is still the daddy of them all. Over seventy years old and still going strong! No unit should be without a pair, the very minimum, and used as a section wherever possible.

Do you miss not having any women around?
There's a time and place for everything. Between contracts we can live like kings. Women are expensive toys, or as the Poles say, the relaxation of warriors! If we should fall in love we might even have to think again about giving up this way of life. Perish the thought!

Do you see a role for mercenary soldiers as garrison troops?
Never. First of all they are too expensive for such a passive
role and secondly they would make a damned nuisance of
themselves in no time through sheer boredom.

*What are your views on a conscripted army as opposed to a
volunteer army?*
Soldiering is a highly professional occupation. It takes five
years training before a man can really call himself a soldier.
It seems more intelligent to us that a national army should
consist of well-paid professional volunteer soldiers, carefully
chosen men who in time of war would form the nucleus of a
corps of instructors to a new civilian army who would then
have to be conscripted. But in peacetime a conscripted army
must contain, inevitably, some proportion of men who hate
soldiering and are totally unsuited to that way of life. Governments should take cognisance of that basic fact. Leave
peacetime soldiering to the professionals and volunteers. In
any case taking large numbers of men out of industry for a
period of perhaps two years must disturb the economy of a
country adversely.

But one of them had a contrary view. He felt that a short
period of conscription, say six months, would enrich the
manhood of a nation, teach it discipline and work off some
of the animal high spirits which seem to be overflowing
everywhere through sheer frustration and lack of excitement. It was, he thought, in the nature of man to be aggressive, to be a hunter. He quoted Burton: 'Peace is the dream
of the wise. War is the history of man.' Now that the atom
bomb had ensured that world wars were a thing of the past,
there must be some other outlet for man's aggressive nature.
If there wasn't, the result must be some eruption, riots
perhaps, as young men found it necessary to let off steam.

[How right he was. Since then we have lived to see football
hooliganism, rent-a-crowd and lately anti-poll-tax demon-
strations in the UK, in most cases manifestations of the need
and urge for excitement and danger. In earlier times wars
absorbed that requirement. It may be of interest to note that
the average age of the rebel Simbas in the Congo rebellion
was around twelve and thirteen. It is the same in the South
African township riots of recent times. The vast majority of
them are in it for kicks; very few of them understand the

political implications of their actions.]

Can you make suggestions for training?
We agree with you that every soldier must begin by being an expert in weapons of all sorts, must be a hundred per cent fit and must know how to dig. Assuming that the training programme caters for this basic training, the next step should be the use of sand-table exercises to teach tactics, the giving of orders and administration of small units. Then there should be field games, one unit against another, the situation having been devised and laid out on a sand table beforehand. The tactical options should be discussed and debated at length before any unit takes to the field to put them into practice. Good fun and nothing like it to teach junior leaders the art of leadership.

Do you feel the lack of courses?
Yes. The technical aspect of soldiering is getting more involved every day. It is the day of the specialist. If we were in a regular army, we would have to choose the branch we wanted to follow. Here we have a feeling the modern world is leaving us behind.

What do you feel when you are described as 'merchants of death'?
Not much. We have given up reading the garbage produced by the gutter press, written mostly by ignorant bums or transient scribblers on their way to a better-paid job. Very few of them take the trouble to research their material. Many seem to write for the effect they think will be popular with their readers. Sadly it usually is.

Are there any weapons that you think should be outlawed?
If such a thing were possible, yes. Napalm for one. Flame-throwers for another. And all chemical weapons, including gas. But keep the atom bomb and its derivatives. They must be the only sure guarantee against World War III.

What do you think the CO should have done with the rapists of nuns that we captured in Oriental province and whom the nuns identified later?
Call for volunteers to cut off their balls publicly. Preferably with a rusty bayonet.

How do you find the officers in the Armée Nationale Congolaise?
OK. Good drinking mates but they don't seem to know much

about soldiering. Worse than that, they don't particularly want to learn. Their interests seem to be elsewhere. The majority of them seem to be more ambitious on a political level.

And the enlisted men of the ANC?
Sad. The Katangese seem to be a cut above the others but the majority of them don't seem to take a pride in being soldiers. I don't think we would either if we got paid as little as they do. What's in it for them? The best they can hope for is to come out of it in one piece.

How do you feel about losing your passport or your nationality because you enlisted as a mercenary soldier in a foreign army?
With respect, sir, you've got the facts wrong. There is no law in the UK which prohibits a soldier from enlisting in a foreign army as a mercenary soldier. The Diplock Report confirmed that. It is unlikely that parliament will seek to change the law.

20

The Great Lukuga Yacht Race

I had been invited to the Navy House for their concert. 'The Navy House' was the name given to the building which housed those members of Tom's navy who were not 'at sea'. At the moment there was little activity on the lake, so most of the men were in residence. They slept in hammocks – which helped convince them they were real sailors, though it did nothing for the older hands, who developed a permanent rick in the back as a result.

The concert was a creditable effort but not remarkable for the talent on display. There was the usual songster on 'the Road to Mandalay', the usual hairy-legged critter in drag prancing around to the tune of the Sugar Plum fairy, and an unusual barber-shop quartet who sang 'Ragtime Cowboy Joe' with an unexpected zing, easily the best item on the bill. And most surprising of all an actual fairy who did conjuring tricks. How he got into the Navy I never discovered, but Tom said he was a good seaman, and it was traditional in the navy, wasn't it?

For the occasion they had invited some of the Congolese dignitaries and their wives, resplendent in elaborate headdresses, several Belgian officers of the headquarters staff, some Indian shopkeepers and two Greek businessmen. When the show was over, the two Greeks invited Tom and me back to their house for a late-night supper and some retsina. They were in fact Greek Cypriots who had crossed over from Tanganyika and settled in the Congo some years before. Cypriots had been made welcome in Tanganyika when it was a British colony, as owners of hotels, managers of country stores, general traders and sisal farmers.

I have always been fond of Greeks, the majority of those I

know having vivid, outgoing personalities, tending to be worldly-wise, hospitable and suave, while at the same time somewhat ruthless in their affairs with women. But the outstanding characteristic of all those Greeks I have met in the past, especially seafaring ones, is that they lead the field in the gambling stakes. The only race that seems to come anywhere near them in this pursuit is the Chinese.

Greeks occupy an anomalous position in shipping circles: they are the owners of a large proportion of the world's maritime transport without themselves being very famous sailors. Since time immemorial – well, shall we say since biblical times anyway, the Greek sailor at sea has been notable chiefly for keeping the land well within sight. It is a matter of record that in the Aegean and its contiguous seas he has developed an endearing ability to dodge behind an island whenever the winds blow incontinently. These considerations were passing lightly through my mind as Tom and I settled into comfortable chairs around the stove in our new friends' kitchen.

I cannot reproduce their surnames with any accuracy but I remember that we called one of them Tarkis and the other answered to Theo. By eleven that night we had lowered a sizeable quantity of their native drink, which I had never tried before, when both of them began to look extremely handsome and likeable chaps.

Tarkis was no mean chef. His hobby was food and the preparation thereof, which probably accounted for his stout frame and happy demeanour. In due course he prepared fillets of steak done in the Belgian way; that is to say, well seasoned and garlicked, if there is such a word, before throwing them into a pan of boiling hot olive oil for a maximum of fifteen seconds – result, outside burnt black, inside practically raw. To this he added a chunk of butter, some *sauce béarnaise*, a handful of matchstick potatoes and a side helping of fresh green lettuce suitably garnished. All done in our presence, so that by the time it was ready we were ravenously hungry and flushed with the wine of Cyprus which they poured straight from a sixteen-litre demijohn.

At some fateful stage of the proceedings Tom asked the Greeks if they were, or had been in more settled times, members of the Albertville Yacht Club. I recalled seeing one or two sad-looking masts sticking up behind a low wall somewhere near the Lukuga river, which was probably all that was left of the yacht club. Tom, as I knew of old, had a general loathing of yacht clubs and their reputedly rarefied members, so I assumed he asked the question out of general interest.

But he had tweaked a nerve. Not only were they yachtsmen; they were also seamen, and proud of it. In their distant past they had served in Greek freighters, one as a cook, the other as a purser. As both these appointments are reputed to hold out the promise of early retirement, we were able readily to appreciate the steps by which they had mounted to their present affluent positions here on the shores of Lake Tanganyika. In short, they conducted their own highly lucrative business supplying the Congolese National Army, and perhaps the rebels too, although I was never sure on this point, with all those things deemed necessary to prosecute a small war. A sort of ship's chandlers you might say. They confessed they had no problem with supply ex-Tanganyika, Northern Rhodesia, Uganda and other places hard by. Their major headache, which I could readily comprehend having trod that road lately as OC 5 Commando, was ultimate payment by the Armée Nationale Congolaise – 'ultimate' being the *mot juste*.

However, both were affluent to that degree of ostentation which is admired by Greeks worldwide, and witnessed in this case by diamond rings on both hands, heavy gold wristchains and emerald stick pins. It became them. On an Englishman such adornment would have looked absurd – flashy, we would have said, but on the Greeks the jewellery was entirely right and proper and served to complement their swarthy good looks, immaculate linen, well-kept hands, oleaginous hair and ability to speak fluently in several obscure languages.

'Yachting, you say,' said Tarkis. 'Do you guys know anything about yachting?'

We laughed. Tom looked at me in a knowing way. How absurd, he seemed to say, we invented it! Tom had built his own twenty-five-foot sloop in New Guinea and sailed it across the Indian Ocean to Durban harbour single handed. I was the proud owner of a thirty-six-foot Norwegian gaff-cutter named after the famous Colin Archer. Its eight-foot bowsprit was feared from Durban Bay to Lourenço Marques and beyond, yea, even into the Mozambique Channel. Did we know about yachting? We most certainly did. Why?

'Like to go for a sail then?'

'Yes, yes! When? Where? How?'

'We've got two sailing boats near our warehouse, just by the yacht club. Nobody ever takes them out these days.'

'Bad, very,' I said. 'Bordering on the sinful. What are they, dinghies?'

'No, no. Proper sailing boats. About thirty-five, forty feet.'

'Wow! Keelers!' said Tom. 'Sloop rigged?'

Theo was not sure of the English term to describe their rigging and side-stepped that one.

'Well, what sails have they got?' pressed Tom. Whenever he had a few drinks he became assertive, sometimes aggressive.

'Mainsail and jib and a smaller one on the stern.'

'Mizzen. You mean a ketch.'

'Do I? OK, ketch then, if you say so. Do you think you could manage a boat like that?' There was a slight deprecatory tone in his voice which energized Tom's antennae unfavourably.

Manage it? Of course he could manage it. He doubted if there was anyone within a thousand miles of us who could manage one better. The retsina was talking. But it resulted in an immediate riposte.

'OK then, smart guy,' said Theo, who was beginning to find Tom a little abrasive. 'How about a race?'

'Certainly, any time.' Tom looked at me for approval, as if to say 'Bloody Greeks! We'll show them a thing or two.'

'Right then,' said Tarkis. 'From the Lukuga river bridge to the buoy and back again. First one to reach the Lukuga river is the winner.'

'Oi! Hold on a minute, mate,' said Tom. 'Where's the buoy?'

'About sixteen miles out, due east of the yacht club. It marks the international border on the lake. It's fifteen feet high with a flashing light, red, every five seconds. You can't miss it.'

'Maybe,' I said, those famous last words being engraved indelibly in my yachting psyche, 'but that won't be enough. Have you got a chart?'

Of course they had, and a compass, and anything else we

might want.

Tom looked at me for agreement in principle. I nodded.

'OK. Next week then, but you must give us a chance to get used to the boat. Once that's settled we can talk about the stakes.'

Now their eyes really glistened. A gamble! This was the stuff that ran in their veins. The local money was of no value in this part of the world; there was nothing you could buy with it. As a medium of exchange it defied all the laws of economics and ran a miserable second to the meaningful things of life like whisky and wine. US dollars, the currency of the mercenary soldier's world, would have been acceptable, of course, but they knew we had no hard money. However, we had something much more valuable to them than that, and which mere money, hard or otherwise, could not buy – small arms!

After a lot of haggling which would have disgraced Ladbroke's, we settled the wager. If we won, they would give us five cases of Scotch whisky. If they won, we would give them two AK47 rifles, complete with two boxes of 762 ammunition, a thousand rounds in each. As all of these things had been captured from the enemy, their disappearance from the armoury would cause us no inconvenience. A little irregular, you might say, but at that time of night it was a circumstance which passed unnoticed. The wager was reduced painfully to writing.

Finally I insisted in a haze of alcohol and bonhomie that the race should be run according to Royal Ocean Racing Club rules, which they had never heard of. Neither had I, of course, but it sounded right and proper at the time. They countered by suggesting the rules of the Royal Piraeus Yacht Club, which they said were more fitting as they were Greeks and the fixture was after all on their home ground. In our cheerful stupor we agreed to this with much back-slapping, neither party being in the slightest way conversant with said rules. Native caution prompted me at the last minute to suggest that we should appoint referees with whom the stakes must be lodged before the race. This was agreed. All that remained was to set the administrative details, which could wait till the next morning. They would introduce us formally to the boats at noon.

Feeling a little used up, Tom and I sauntered down to the

yacht club the following morning. Theo and Tarkis were waiting for us, fresh as two plastic daisies. They led us to a warehouse on the water's edge. We clapped eyes on one of the boats for the first time.

'Seven bastards!' shouted Tom. It was his favourite way of expressing deep concern. When I considered all the other great Australian adjectives at his disposal, I was of course impressed with his moderation.

'Call that a flaming yacht?'

'Yes,' said Tarkis, affronted. 'Why, don't you know how to sail it?'

'Of course I do. But you told us you had two identical ketches. You don't call this a ketch, do you?'

'Well, perhaps not, but you're the one that called it a ketch, and in any case what's all this ketch business? It's a boat, isn't it? It sails, doesn't it? It'll do just as well for an experienced sailor like you, won't it?'

Tom and I looked a little crestfallen. Our brave words of the night before had bounced back in our faces. What we were looking at, can you believe it, was an ancient felucca! A ruddy old Arab trading vessel such as you see on postcards of the Nile. Neither of us had actually seen, never mind handled, a felucca before in our lives. The Greeks grinned at our apparent discomfiture.

'Don't worry,' said Theo, 'we'll teach you how to sail them.'

That was the last straw. Tom answered with something stronger than his usual quota of illegitimate offspring.

We examined the craft. 'Unique' is the only word which would describe them fairly. They were massive affairs more than forty feet long, with a beam of about ten feet. They looked as though they might be thirty feet on the waterline, with a lengthy sloping overhang fore and aft, typical Arab construction of an age long past. They must have been eighty or ninety years old. More maybe.

'African teak,' said Tom, beginning to take a professional interest in their construction, running his hand along a gunwhale. 'Could be iroko. Look at that! Can you beat it? The strakes are held together with coir stitching!'

The stitch holes were about two inches from the edge of the strakes. Whatever we thought about them as yachts, they were undoubtedly works of a bygone art. We examined the hulls. They were still in excellent condition, well covered with an anti-fouling composition and apparently free from worm and rot. But for two men expecting the fine lines of a racing yacht they were a grave disappointment.

The only saving grace was that the two boats were identical and we could take our pick. We chose *Sinbad*. Theo and Tarkis had the other one, called *Sohar*.

We climbed on board. Two main crossbeams supported the main mast partner on either side and took the weight of a forty-foot forward-sloping main mast. It had probably been shaped from a single tree trunk. The mizzen mast, which stood vertically, was about twenty feet high. Both masts were well stayed with powerful shrouds. I supposed boats like these could have carried about thirty tons of cargo in their day with ease. Tom tried to examine the garboard strakes but gave it up, muttering there was too much sand-bagged ballast on top of the keelson. The blocks were all handmade and wooden throughout, shells, pins and sheaves. The block for raising the mainsail had a power of eight and was about two feet long and eighteen inches wide. That would have to be treated with some respect. A crack on the nut from that lad would end our sailing days for ever.

We familiarized ourselves with the running rigging, which was simple and strong. The mainsail was, of course, the age-old triangular lateen job and made of heavy cotton can-vas with its edges roped all round, and stiff as all get out. The main spar which ran diagonally across the main mast was about forty feet long and seized in the middle to the hounds, with one end secured to the deck. The other end stuck up into the sky at an angle of 45 degrees. Tom reckoned the sail might be as big as 800 square feet, a terrifying thought. The jib boom jutted out from the stem about eight feet, and a running tackle carried the headsail tack out to its far end. Everything, as became this well-tried design, was im-mensely strong, simple and workable.

'We'll need a big crew,' said Tom, pronouncing judge-ment.

'Ten men in each boat,' said Tarkis.

'Agreed.'

'No holds barred. OK?'

'What do you mean "no holds barred"? ' asked Tom, on guard.

'Well … we can row if we have to. Sometimes there's no wind. And things like that.'

Sounded a bit strange to our naïve ears but we accepted the terms.

'Righty-oh!' said Tom. 'But no outboard motors, none of that mullarkey. Windpower and manpower only. OK?'

'OK. Windpower and manpower only.'

We shook hands on it, bowing our heads never so slightly to witness the solemn pact.

Tom and I spent the rest of the morning rigging the boat, checking its equipment and wondering how the hell one sailed a thing like this. Tom said it would be no problem. The prevailing winds were south-west and north-east. Our course was due east and then due west. We could use these winds to give us a quartering breeze, perhaps even a beam wind, which should push us along at three or four knots. At the worst he reckoned she might get within 70 degrees of the wind if she had to. The important thing was to get some men to scrub the bottom clean before we put her back in the water and give her time to make up. Words of wisdom. So we did that *jaldi jaldi*.

The race was scheduled to begin the following Sunday from a start line on the lake side of the Lukuga bridge. It is here that the Lukuga river pours wantonly out of the lake to flow due westward for about 250 kilometres until it joins the Lualaba river, which becomes the mighty Congo further north. We had a few days to get used to the eccentricities of a felucca and, if there was time, to try her out on the lake. There wasn't. There never is. Our first task then was to choose a crew. Of seasoned yachtsmen, ancient mariners and chancers, there was apparently no dearth. However, by the time we had unmasked the *soi-disant* members of the Royal Yacht Squadron, Cowes, and the Royal Thames Yacht Club, Westminster, we were left with one man who had actually hired a sailing dinghy on the Serpentine one August Bank holiday in his youth. The other nine members of the crew were recruited via Tom's press gang.

But given the numbers now involved as crew, the stakes had to be upped. We finally agreed on ten cases of Scotch whisky on their side against six Kalashnikov rifles plus 4,000 rounds of ammo on ours. Magnanimously we allowed Theo and Tarkis to choose their crew from those ex-members of the prestigious yacht clubs aforesaid who failed to come up to our exacting standard.

Enthusiasm for the race ran riot in our barracks and spread like wildfire in the town. In no time at all the horse-racing fraternity in 5 Commando (some of whom had enlisted to escape the wrath of unhappy bookies) got wind of the event, and two genuine bookmakers emerged. They erected their stands on the steps of the cathedral and accepted bets from townspeople and members of the unit alike.

One of the bookmakers was Lieutenant Ron Columbic, the son of a famous Johannesburg bookie. He questioned Tom and me exhaustively on the merits of *Sinbad* and our reputed but possibly suspect yachting prowess. After which he assessed our chances, enquired wistfully if there was any possibility of fixing the race for a consideration yet to be determined, and established regretfully there was not. Impressed no doubt with the good opinion we held of ourselves and Tom's seafaring background, he opened the betting by offering ten to one against *Sohar*. I thought this was a bit extravagant for the unknown quantities involved and cautioned him not to do his boots out of a mistaken loyalty to the unit.

Meanwhile the other bookie, Volunteer Jimmy Bishop – alias the Saint – was offering fifteen to one against us in *Sinbad*. 'Jim always pays!' his board said. 'He'll bloody well pay this time too,' said Tom, chagrined by the long odds against the home crew. On the strength of it he backed *Sinbad* to win himself 30,000 Congolese francs just to teach the Saint a lesson.

Enthusiasm spilled over into the town, and it was hard to find anybody, from the archbishop down to the hospital orderlies, who had not backed their fancy one way or the other. For a spell the war was forgotten.

The great day dawned. The race was scheduled to start at 0600 hours. A huge crowd lined both banks of the river and hung over the iron railings of the bridge, dropping things into the water – presumably to see how fast the river was flowing.

The referees were Major Alistair Wicks, representing us, and Colonel Albert Kakuji, representing them – 'them' for this purpose being the townspeople of Albertville. The popular colonel, whom one could never have mistaken for a retiring wallflower, arrived in gala dress seated somewhat insecurely in a howdah strapped atop a small and docile elephant, and attended by about one hundred chanting warriors from the local garrison, all suitably armed with spears and beating tom-toms for the occasion. The little Jumbo was unmoved. Under his red and gold head-covering, his minuscule but knowing eye seemed to say that he had seen worse things in his time, but not much. The colonel was heard to tell the local press that yes, he enjoyed riding the elephant, it was like, like... *comment dirai-je*? ... a portable grandstand.

Two stakes were then erected on opposite banks of the Lukuga where it ran out of the lake, to mark the start line. Then Major Wicks warned the two feluccas through a faulty public address system to keep to the bridge side of the start line until the first gun had sounded. This official announcement gave the proceedings some authenticity, despite the fact nobody could understand what Alistair was saying, the reception being too crackly. Even so, it galvanized the crowd into breathless anticipation while reassuring the punters that this was in fact a properly conducted race. The first gun would indicate that we were under starter's orders, so to speak, and that we had ten minutes to line up for the actual start, when there would be a second gun, after which we could cross the line.

As Tom hated racing of any kind at sea, I was named skipper of *Sinbad* and Tom became sailing master. There was only the lightest of light breezes blowing, thank heavens, as we were towed up to the bridge and our umbilical cord was cut free. Tom then gave orders for the massive mainsail yard to be raised. With a squealing of blocks fit to wake the dead the mainsail rose with an awful bending of the yard and we belayed the halyard. That left about five miles of rope on the deck. The mizzen followed and then the headsail. Everything stood limp and inert above and in a hell of a mess below. Now there wasn't a breath of wind. 'Out sweeps!' shouted Tom, whereupon the crew produced half a dozen bamboo poles from below, as though unveiling some secret weapon. They started to row after a fashion and finally with much yelling and cursing got us to point more or less in the right direction. Meantime I was waggling the tiller in the hope that it would encourage a little forward movement, but uncertain as to whether this was permitted under RORC rules or not. In the event it proved lifeless and singularly ineffective. I persuaded myself I only did it to show who was nominally in command, and not with any evil intent.

Ten minutes later the starting gun sounded and the race was under way. The crowd roared as we crawled over the start line propelled by manpower alone and, I felt quite sure, the fervent hopes of a thousand well-wishers who knew they were on to a good thing.

Our course was due east for sixteen miles. If we made three knots, we should be back here to claim our prize in about ten hours. Of course we would win; there was never any doubt about that in our minds; the race was a mere formality, a quaint ritual to go through before we drank the winnings.

As soon as we were well out on the lake and clear of the headlands we picked up a slant, a gentle, honeyed breeze, steady if modest. The lateen sails swelled, settled into a beautiful curve and began to draw us along handsomely at about two knots. (Three knots was written off as unbridled optimism.) Everything creaked agreeably as the old boat heeled very slightly to one side. An occasional puff of wind caused the reefing points to patter on the sail like rain, bringing a spiritual solace to the soul. The ship leaked abominably but the crew felt no end of sea-dogs, apprehensive and worried-looking sea-dogs, but sea-dogs nevertheless.

Sohar meanwhile was about two or three cables north of us and from the appalling noise the crew were making appeared to be enjoying themselves hugely. 'Drunken bums,' said Tom, accurately. Later it transpired that the Greeks had seen fit to bring spirituous liquors on board to bribe the crew into greater efforts. In *Sinbad* the severest mild discipline reigned, Tom walking fore and aft with a rope's end held menacingly in one hand, shouting Australian encouragement at the wind.

The morning wore on, the wind freshened and we drew steadily ahead of *Sohar*, as expected. Tom and I attributed this to our superior seamanship and plain know-how. 'Experience always tells', said Tom modestly. I agreed. About noon Tom sent a likely lad up the mainmast to see if he could spot the buoy. Half-way up the silly bugger lost his handhold amid much laughter and fell into the lake, so that we had to round up into the wind to fish him out, losing valuable time.

However, before his fall he said he was certain he could see the flashing buoy straight ahead, but did we know *Sohar* was gaining on us by using its sweeps? We didn't, but we were not worried, sweeps having been permitted in terms of the RORC and Royal Piraeus Yacht Club rules we had fashioned jointly. Anybody who could push an old tub like this along with manpower was entitled to every yard they made, was the gist of our thinking.

About one o'clock we reached the buoy. To round it and go onto the other tack presented the sailing master with an insuperable difficulty, nobody having the vaguest idea of the drill involved. He decided to play it safe and lowered the main and then the mizzen, manhandled them around onto the new tack and raised them again amid uproarious laughter, many of the crew having in the meantime succumbed to the powerful effects of Simba beer drunk in the heat of the day. Mercifully avoiding a capsize, the lateen sail filled again and we settled down to a gentle zephyr slightly forward of abeam which carried us somewhat north of our true course. This had the makings of trouble to come but as the breeze kept us moving Tom and I decided we would hold the course and make a board once we could see the finish.

Sohar had now rounded the buoy and appeared to be closing the gap between us without the use of their sweeps; lake breezes are notoriously local and sometimes, as now, favour the less adroit. Meanwhile we broke out the midday rations, our old friends rice, sardines and biscuits, washed down with more beer. About five in the afternoon both boats were well north of but within sight of the Lukuga bridge and the finish line and thus found it necessary to go about, a manoeuvre fraught with peril and latent disaster. The wind had freshened slightly to about Force 4 which made the change of course interesting if not downright dangerous. But we managed it. After bestowing on us a heady little gallop at three to four knots, the breeze promptly died. At six o'clock both feluccas were about 800 yards from the finish line and becalmed. Both crews were too sozzled to use their sweeps, and the best their skippers could get out of them was a spirited rendering of 'What shall we do with the drunken sailor' from *Sinbad* and 'O Shenandoah, I love your daughter' from *Sohar*, neither of which influenced the sails in any way. We were now within hailing distance of each other and thus able to advise and insult as we thought fit.

As *Sinbad* was very slightly to windward, I was confident we would cross the finish line first, even if we had to wait till midnight to do it. But I reckoned without the ingenuity of the Greeks, both of whom now stood on the stern of *Soha*r drinking our good health ostentatiously. But why was Tarkis talking into something which looked like a PRC 10 transmitter with its aerial up? We couldn't guess.

Suddenly, in the gathering dusk and out of nowhere I thought I could hear the umistakable thrash of a chopper! I was right. A few seconds later our Bell helicopter hove in sight about a mile out in the lake and quite close to the water. Undoubtedly it was piloted by Capitaine Alphonse Legris, a French Canadian. Too late I appreciated the dastardly act which was about to unfold before our very eyes. Too late I realized the full import of that matey little booze-up between the Greeks and the redoubtable pilot which Tom and I had witnessed only the night before.

'I lives to see it!' screamed Tom, adding emphatically of course the usual crèche of offspring born out of wedlock.

And see it we did. Down came the helicopter, hovered discreetly behind *Sohar* and pushed her along at a steady three knots until she crossed the finish line, cheered all the way by her useless crew of layabouts to be proclaimed winner of the Great Lukuga Yacht Race by the referees. Perhaps they had understood, better than Tom and I, the meaning of the clause 'No holds barred: manpower and wind power only!'

I commiserated with Ron Columbic, who had lost a packet on the race. The Saint on the other hand had cleaned up and, typically, hence his nickname, was spending the winnings on all and sundry.

The AK47s and the ammunition were duly handed over by the referees to the Greeks, and a wild night ensued. You would have thought from the stories floating around the various bars in Albertville that night that *Sohar* had won the Fastnet in record time. Certainly the crew of *Sinbad* felt cheated of their victory on a technicality. But Tom and I were not finished yet.

The following day the Greeks tried out the guns and declared, somewhat aggrieved, that they were faulty and would not fire. Whereupon Tom examined them only to find, – *mirabile dictu*! – that some dastardly person or persons unknown had removed their firing pins. 'Whoever would do such a thing?' he asked me with a wink. However, he kept this special knowledge to himself, content with informing Theo and Tarkis that there appeared to be some small technical problem which he was sure the armourer could solve very rapidly – but it would cost them.

The price, need I tell you, was ten cases of Scotch whisky.

21

The Light at Faradje

The events which took place in Stanleyville on the morning
of 24 November 1964 shocked the entire civilized world. As
soon as news reached the rebel command that Belgian paratroops were on their way to rescue the hostages, their fate
was sealed. One hundred and fifteen of them were paraded
outside the Victoria Hotel and ruthlessly gunned down in
cold blood. The Belgians came, they rescued their nationals
and they departed. 5 Commando, the strike force of an
independent brigade, were left to get on with the job of
rounding up the rebels and pacifying the population.

As soon as some sort of law and order had been reintro-
duced, we began to put our minds to the rescue of the
remaining hostages. They were distributed in missions all
over Oriental province, an area greater than that of France.
For this purpose I was asked to send 54 Commando, under
Lieutenant Joe Wepener, to Paulis, a major city some 400
kilometres north of Stanleyville. Two weeks later he reported
that his unit had rescued over a hundred missionaries,
priests and nuns from Wamba, a large town ninety
kilometres south of Paulis. Joe had done well. Shortly afterwards he sent me this letter.

> Dear Major,
> I attach my official report on the capture of Wamba and the
> release of the hostages. I thought I would write you this
> personal note as well to let you know how things are going
> with us and bring one or two things to your notice.
> I have set up our HQ in the Brewery here in Paulis but as
> some sod has flogged most of the sugar we are not able to get
> the plant going at anything like its proper capacity. But trust
> me, we will. Meantime we're not thirsty!

First of all, about the hostages. I wish you could have seen them. They were in a shocking state when we finally got them out. Some of those Simba bastards had been raping and ill treating the nuns night after night. I needn't tell you we sorted them out good and proper when we got hold of them. When I got the women back here they knelt in the brewery yard and thanked God for their delivery. One or two of my blokes started to cry, silly buggers. I was ashamed of them. I asked some of the ladies why God had let them get into the hands of the Simbas in the first place.

Among the hostages we rescued from Wamba was a little party named Helen Roseveare who I think must be OC the Protestant missionaries in this part of the world. She would have made a bloody good soldier! She is a doctor and one of the most amazing people I ever met in my life. The brave Simbas knocked her about something cruel as well, she was black and blue all over. She forgave them, can you believe it? She's only about two bricks high but made of iron. She told me she has a secret weapon – invincible faith, whatever that is. God bless her anyway. I had my photo taken with her, it was an honour. I hope that's OK with you.

I enclose a nominal roll of the hostages we sent on to Stanleyville today in a C130, *en route* for Leo. As you will see we are still short a very large number of them. The general opinion here among the Belgians is that we will never see any of them alive again, but it is always possible some could have been taken up north to Aba or Aru where I believe the rebels have a strong base.

The other thing is: some of the men are giving me a hard time about their pay. The main gripe is about the half of the half. The half of our pay which we get in Congolese francs isn't worth a damn, as you know, and there's nothing to buy locally with it anyway. The option in the contract which allows us to transfer half of the amount we get in Congolese francs into hard currency at the end of our contract is what they're beefing about. They want that altered so that they can send all of it out in US dollars. They reckon that will make things fairer because they say they didn't know anything about the Congolese mickey mouse money when they signed the contract. Hope you will be able to visit us soon and sort something out as I don't think I can keep them quiet much longer.

We brought a lot of suitcases and things back from Wamba which belonged to the hostages. Some of them were unclaimed when the missionaries went off this morning. I have been through most of them, clothes etc, nothing of any great

value, but in one suitcase I found someone's diary. No name
or address in it. I showed it around before they went but
nobody claimed it. I am sending it to you with this letter. I
haven't had time to read it as to tell you the truth I don't seem
to have much time for anything at the moment. Other than
getting the brewery going again that is, ha, ha. Only joking.
My regards to Commandant Wicks,
Obediently,
Joe Wepener. Lt.
OC 54 Commando. Paulis.
31 Dec 64.

Early in January 1965 I was granted fourteen days leave. I
spent this in Durban, Natal, most of it sailing my thirty-six-
foot gaff-rigged cutter *Colin Archer* or just basking in the
brilliant sunshine, trying to forget the horrors I had lived
through in the past few months. But when boredom finally
set in I remembered the diary Joe had sent me and began to
read it. It had been written by a young woman missionary,
a doctor. It was riveting. And heart-breaking, at the same
time. It enlightened me considerably on what had been
happening on the rebel side during our advance from
Kamina base to Stanleyville. Whoever the writer was, she
was plainly a person of tremendous faith in Almighty God.
Her conviction that, come what may, she would survive to
glorify His name and do His bidding in her missionary work
in the Congo shone through the tragic pages like a laser
beam. There was no doubt she had suffered agonies for her
faith. Possibly even death.

I gleaned one or two facts about the writer from the diary.
After leaving high school she had studied at a Bible college.
It was after this training that she had decided to dedicate her
life to the Lord as a missionary. Then she had studied at
Baylor University medical school at Waco, Texas, for several
years, obtained her MD and completed her internship locally. She had been accepted by the Africa Inland Mission as
soon as a vacancy occurred and sent out to the Oriental
Province of the Congo.

But as to her name there was no clue. She referred to her
colleagues by one initial only. As she was one of two doctors
at her mission I assumed it must be a fairly big one. No doubt
when the whole area was pacified, which might take a very
long time by the look of it, I could find out who she was and

return the diary to her, if she was still alive. I thought seriously of destroying it, because of its contents, but decided in the end to keep it safely until events had had a chance to unfold.

In the main she gave a graphic description of the political storm which burst about her head in July and August 1964, the course of the rebellion and the events of the next three months which were finally to wreck the mission and the lives of every member of it, staff, patients and pupils alike. Most tragic of all she gave a detailed description of how she was raped by the leader of the Simba gang who had looted their mission.

Four months had passed and 5 Commando was now in Bunia, a major city in the north-eastern corner of Oriental province, near Lake Albert. Bunia had been the scene of heavy fighting last November. The Armée Populaire de Libération, the rebel army, had withdrawn to this far corner of the Congo and were continuing to defy the central government. My unit, in support of the Congolese National Army, was to be used in suppressing the rebellion. We had mustered at Kamina and flown to Bunia in the last few days and were settling in once more to training. The climate here was cool and bracing, the terrain open and hilly at an average one thousand metres above sea-level. It was a welcome change from the fetid jungles along the Congo river we knew too well. Bunia was a good station.

As I always did, I made a point of interviewing each man personally on his arrival in the unit. The last man to see me had flown in that morning from Léopoldville. He was an American. He said he had made his own way from the United States to join 5 Commando. This was most unusual. His name was Mark McRory. He looked like an all-American full back, stood well over six foot and must have weighed more than 200 pounds. He was fresh faced and boyish-looking, with very close-cropped hair.

'You are an American, McRory?'

'Yes, Colonel.'

'May I see your passport?'

He handed it to me. It said he was twenty-seven years of age and had been born in Austin, Texas.

'Does the US military attaché in Léo know you are here?'

'No, sir. I would rather he did not know.'

'I am told that US nationals run the risk of losing their passport and other terrible things if they enlist under a foreign flag. Do you know about that?'

'Yes, I do. But I am prepared to take that risk.'

'OK then, as long as you know. What is your previous military service?'

'I am a lieutenant in the US Marine Corps.'

'You are what!' I nearly fell off my chair.

'I am a lieutenant in the US Marine Corps. I graduated as an officer at West Point Military Academy in 1959. I have been serving at the Marines Depot in Washington since then.'

'Have you any army papers?'

'I have, of course, but I didn't think it wise to bring them with me.'

I whistled. Could he be telling the truth? More likely he had been cashiered for some offence.

'Have you resigned then?'

'No, sir. I am still a serving officer. I have obtained a special furlough.'

'Like language leave, for instance?'

'No. I made an application to my commandant on exceptional grounds and he agreed to let me go for six months.'

'May I know more about those special grounds? I hope for your sake you didn't think we could teach you anything here, because if you do, I am afraid you are going to be greatly disappointed. This is a very minor show as wars go ... '

'No, I understand that, sir. It wasn't that. Something else entirely. I would prefer to keep my reasons a secret, if it's all the same to you.'

'I'm sorry, but that's not really possible. I have to know them if you want to join my unit. But I can assure you your secret will be safe with me.'

He began again, a little reluctantly.

'A very dear friend of mine was a member of the African Inland Mission. She was reported missing last November when the Stanleyville massacre occurred. She had been in the Congo for just over a year, at a mission near Paulis. She is a very special person to me, and I intend to do everything I can to try and find her, or to find out what has happened to her, if that is humanly possible.'

'Can you tell me something about her?'

'Yes. She is a missionary doctor. Her name is Marylou Daintree. She is twenty-five. That is one of the last photographs ever taken of her.'

He handed me a well-thumbed snapshot. It showed an extremely attractive girl with short blonde hair, dressed in a white housecoat, the sort doctors wear when doing their rounds on the wards. She was holding a black baby who was pulling at the stethoscope around her neck. A thatched-roof building was in the background. It could have been part of a mission hospital.

'That's her. That photograph was taken at a place called Mungbere.'

'Yes, I know it. It's not far from Paulis. But hold on a minute, Mark. Just let me have a look at a list of missing persons your military attaché gave me in Léo a few days ago.'

I fished it out of a drawer.

'Rev'd and Mrs Holte, Norwegian Mission, Bili,' it began. Then it listed twelve or more persons, mostly missionaries, missing, believed dead. At the bottom of the list I came to 'Dr Marylou Daintree, Africa Inland Mission, last heard of November 1964 at Paulis. Believed dead, but slight possibility may be in Aba area.'

'She's on the list anyway. There it is. Do you know anything more that could be helpful? Any letters she may have sent you just before Stanleyville, for instance.'

'No. Nothing. Sorry.'

'Pity. But first things first. You've come to join 5 Commando because you think we are going to fight in that area. That's it, isn't it?' He nodded. 'And you think that if you are with us you may get a chance to look for her at the same time?'

'Exactly.'

'I admire your guts. You can count on me to help all the way. I'm entirely behind you, but there are problems you probably don't know about. For a start it is by no means certain that we shall succeed in reaching Aba. We simply don't know the strength of the enemy or the support he is receiving down the Nile. It may be much greater than we think. There's some talk of his being assisted by Egyptian mercenary troops. In that case we may have to build up our forces too. That will take time. At the moment we have 500 men in 5 Commando. In addition we have 14 Commando, 200 strong, a Congolese unit with Belgian, German and French mercenary officers. Plus a brigade of the Congolese National Army. Not a big force for such a vast area. The campaign could take months.'

'I'm prepared for that, sir. I want to join your unit in any capacity you see fit. All I ask is that when we are in the Aba area you make it possible for me to search for Marylou.'

'It's a deal Mark.' We shook hands on it. 'Let's talk a little about your military background.'

At the end of half an hour I appreciated my incredible good fortune. Here was an officer from one of the finest fighting outfits in the world, ready, willing and able to serve under me in any capacity I thought fit. I gave him his own commando at once. We agreed he would not mention that he was a serving officer in the US Marine Corps but would merely say that he had been educated at a military school in Canada. That would cover up his accent and his expertise. I advised him on no account to tell anyone he was an American. In the event of his capture, unlikely though that was, it would leak out and mean his certain death. The enemy's attitude towards America was ignorant and rabid, but Canada they had never heard of. Most Congolese I had met thought it was in North Africa. Finally, I said, we must change his name. He now became Forrester, which had been his mother's maiden name. I issued him with a new identity card. This showed his nationality as Canadian. I then took him to the mess and introduced him to Major Wicks and the other officers and left him.

I returned to my office, intrigued with the story Mark McRory had told me. Obviously, I thought, there must be some connection between Marylou Daintree and the diary in my safe. I read it again. The stark horror of everything the writer had experienced in the last few weeks of her life before Stanleyville struck me again, her personal suffering being perhaps the most poignant part of it. Should I show the diary to Lieutenant Forrester? If it was Marylou Daintree's diary, he would certainly know her writing. He would also read her description of the awful thing that had happened to her. If we never saw Marylou again, her diary could only bring him more grief, a grief which would stay with him the rest of his days. If she was still alive and we did find her, by some miracle, perhaps she would not want him, or anyone else, to read her diary or to know what she had suffered. Either way, it seemed to me, there was nothing to be gained by showing it to Mark. It could not help him in any way. I locked it away in my safe.

The unit began its intensive training. Lieutenant Forrester took over his command and welded them into an efficient fighting unit in the course of the next four weeks. He certainly knew his stuff. I was very pleased with him.

My overall plan was to concentrate the brigade at a place called Nioko, one hundred kilometres north of us. This would be my forward base. From there we would advance cautiously, probing the enemy's strength by active patrolling. But a preliminary action would be needed first. Port Mahagi was a small town practically on the Ugandan border at the northern end of Lake Albert. This would have to be in my hands before we could move forward. I had to know that my right flank was safe and free from interference by Ugandan mercenaries. I gave this important operation to Lieutenant Forrester. It involved movement up the lake in barges from Kasenyi in the south to the top end of the lake, a distance of 130 kilometres. The water-borne assault would not be a simple operation, and I was anxious to see what he made of it. Meanwhile the brigade would form an advanced base at Ngote, thirty kilometres north of Nioko.

Lieutenant Forrester put in a spirited attack from the lake four days later. Port Mahagi capitulated. He lost four men wounded but none killed. The bulk of the enemy withdrew in the direction of Uganda. This had given Mark the chance to make his reputation with his men. They knew him now as a fearless leader, and one they would follow through thick and thin.

This advance enabled the main force to move up to Ngote. On the first night the enemy attacked our perimeter and we lost two men killed and several wounded, but patrols reported the next day that the Armée Populaire had decided to withdraw into the foot hills about fifteen kilometres off. They appeared to be in very great number.

A day or two later we had a visit from General Mulamba, who was in overall command of the area. I was able to entertain him to a dinner prepared by one of my men who had been a trained chef. The main dish was roast sucking pig. The general helped me recruit a force of local young men for use as scouts, whom we now christened 'the Black Watch'. When all was in readiness I issued the order to advance on two axes, 5 Commando supported by two battalions of the Congolese National Army on one, 14 Commando and the third battalion on the other.

The terrain on our axis was flat and featureless. It consisted of a single mud road, ditched on both sides, running through cultivated fields of manioc which gave way from time to time to savannah and sand. In the far distance were some low hills. After three hours' march our leading Ferret scout cars came under heavy machine-gun fire from these hills. My troops deployed at once and took cover. I made my way up to the front carefully, using the deep ditch on one side of the road for cover. Once there I scoured the area ahead with my glasses. The enemy seemed to be well dug in. I presumed this would be their first well-prepared line of defence. Meanwhile they were putting down a tremendous volume of small-arms fire. The men were digging in all round me, using anything they could lay their hands on. The enemy had us in enfilade and as there was very little cover available it looked to me as though further forward movement in daylight could be ruled out. But there was the obvious alternative. Remove the enemy first. I sent for Lieutenant Forrester. I had held his unit in reserve for just such an opportunity.

'Mark. The enemy are in some strength about two ks off. I think you can just make them out.'

He focused his binoculars on the general area and picked them up a few seconds later.

'I would say they have at least four heavy machine-guns there and are almost certainly dug in. I want you to destroy them. Attack from the left. Use a wide encircling movement. No hurry. Make a recce of your line of approach and let me know your general plan. You can have two companies of Congolese in support if you wish. I will arrange air and a mortar bombardment to suit your plan.'

He marked the enemy position on his map and went off to make his reconnaissance. I sent for Major Wicks. Alistair was my Air Liaison officer when we were in action. He had direct contact with the airfield at Bunia, where we were supported by two B26s and six T28s. He could talk to the pilots when they were overhead as well. They knew each other of old and had done this sort of thing many times before.

Mark was back in less than an hour and pointed out the route he intended to take and his approximate start line for the final phase. He would assault the enemy position at noon. I co-ordinated the timing. We would begin our 81 mm bombardment at 1145 hours, using yellow smoke once we had the range. This would identify the target. Alistair would lay on a rocket attack by the T28s from 1150 hours until noon. As soon as the planes had fired their last salvos, we would cease fire and Mark would go in.

The operation began and went like clockwork. It was a typical piece of small unit warfare, and thrilling to conduct. Mark had a covered line of approach for most of the way and was unseen by the enemy until about 800 metres from his proposed start line. As soon as the enemy saw him, they switched their fire from us onto him, and his unit went to ground and stayed there.

At 1145 hours we opened up with the 81 mm mortars and awaited the air strike which came in exactly at 1150 hours. Mario Santachez was a highly experienced and fearless pilot, and his Cubans were the cream of the crop. Alistair talked them onto the target. Positive, they said; they could see the yellow smoke. They circled the area once, lined up on the enemy position and came in at about three hundred metres Wham! Whoosh! one after another. Their rockets streaked off in succession, exploding into the hills with a thunderous echo. I focused again on Mark's men. They were moving forward now, running from cover to cover. When the T28s had fired the last of their rockets they circled again and again, coming in lower and lower. They began to strafe the enemy with cannon fire. I was damned glad I was not on the receiving-end of that lot. At exactly noon the planes flew off and we stopped firing in support. I focused again on Mark's position. I could just pick out his men advancing in line abreast, Mark leading them, steadily, under control, bayonets flashing in the sun.

After a few minutes the radio crackled into life.

'Position taken. Consolidating.' It was Mark's voice, calm and precise. He was some soldier.

I gave the order to 5 Commando to advance. The leading troops deployed and advanced on foot, well spread out. It was heavy going through the cassava and abandoned cotton fields, the soft black soil clinging to our boots. Forty minutes later we reached our objective, now held by Mark's men, passed through it and continued on toward Gulu. Our first serious opposition had been overcome. The enemy had suffered eight dead and fourteen wounded. The remainder had withdrawn, abandoning two Vickers .303 medium machine-guns and two Browning .50 heavy machine-guns, all mounted on tripods, still in their gun pits. I added these weapons, which were in perfect condition, to our reserve, plus a vast store of ammunition. I sent for Mark and congratulated him on an excellent piece of work. If this was to be typical of the enemy's resistance, things looked good for a swift advance on Aba. I told him so. That was the best news I could have given him.

In the following three weeks we made astonishing progress, overcoming successive lines of defence one after another, with a minimum of casualties on both sides. The enemy were on the run. The question now was, where would he make his major stand? If we advanced fast enough, we could stop him preparing a strong defensive position. Only one major obstacle in his favour now stood between us and Aba. That was the River Nzoro. The river formed a formidable natural barrier and could be crossed only by an iron bridge one kilometre from a small town named Dramba which stood on the other side of it. If we were unable to capture the bridge, we would have to make a very wide encircling movement on foot. This could take two or three weeks. Alternatively I could ask General Mulamba for some bridge-building equipment and a company of engineers, but as that might have to be flown in from Léopoldville it could take even longer.

That night I spent with the reserve unit and had a chance to talk to Mark.

'What do you think now, Colonel?' asked Mark. 'How many days before we can take Aba?'

'If we're lucky, maybe seven. But that will mean capturing Dramba, frontally, first of all. I'm just weighing up the chances a fast-moving strike force might have of taking the bridge before they can blow it. If we could do that, we could attack the town. Then there would be nothing to stop us on the road to Aba.'

'Great. Why don't you use my commando? We've done

nothing for the last two weeks, and my boys are raring to go.'
I liked to hear him say 'my boys'.

Mark was obviously the best man for the job. It would mean movement by night, which was against my better judgement, but the prize was out of all proportion to the risk involved. We discussed tactics and made a tentative plan. Mark could move out of our forward position some hours before dawn and make a dash for the bridge. If he secured it, the main force could follow up just after daylight, cross the bridge and hit the town. I gave it a lot of thought and decided, all things considered, it was a reasonable risk.

But this was the last time I was going to chance losing Mark. In all fairness he ought to be given the opportunity to do the special work he had planned on doing once we reached Aba. Meanwhile he issued his unit with a warning order for the operation. I watched them blacken up, in great spirits. Mark was due to set off for Dramba at midnight. I had a small private chat with him just before he went. I knew the sort of man he was, his background and his beliefs. I also knew he was facing one hell of a risk.

'You believe in prayer, don't you, Mark?' I asked.

'Sure do, Colonel. We're all Baptists at home. So was ... so is Marylou.'

'Good. I'm a firm believer in prayer too. I'll be praying for you tonight, Mark. You will succeed. I'm sure of it.'

He looked at me as though he was seeing me for the first time. I opened my Bible.

'There's a bit here in Joshua I've just been reading. Could have been written specially for all of us, Mark. "Be strong and of a good courage; be not afraid, neither be thou dismayed: for the Lord thy God is with thee whithersoever thou goest."'

Mark was not afraid. He had the element of surprise. All his unit needed was a bit of luck. They had it. They rushed the defences at Dramba, seized the bridge and held it until daylight came flooding in. 5 Commando arrived shortly afterwards, deployed, attacked the town frontally and captured it before the enemy had time to react. The place was a veritable arsenal and the focal point of all their supply. It contained a vast quantity of arms and ammunition, all of Soviet manufacture. Mark lost two of his men killed and

seven wounded, which saddened us all, but it was a resounding victory.

Our road to Aba was now clear. Lieutenant Forrester,
despite his laid-back temperament – a product of his marine
training, I supposed – was keyed up to a pitch of intense
excitement. Now he was totally preoccupied with his own
problem, living in his own private world. I could read his
mind and guessed exactly how he would pray: Please, Lord,
let me find Marylou safe and well.

There was no stopping 5 Commando now. A few days later
we encircled Aba and captured it with very little resistance.
The enemy had withdrawn at the eleventh hour, in the
direction of Faradje, leaving us to capture over one hundred
prisoners. We consolidated. I sent Mark's unit to the AIM
headquarters, which were situated on a rocky outcrop about
one kilometre north of the town. Then I sent a fighting patrol
to the Sudan border, seventeen kilometres beyond Aba.
After that I established my headquarters in the country club.
Finally, I handed over the town to one battalion of the
Congolese National Army. They would garrison it from now
on.

Mark returned. The mission had been abandoned. There
was not a soul there. The place had been ransacked from top
to bottom. The senseless destruction of doors, windows and
fittings was heart-breaking. The classrooms were devas-
tated, the chapel was vandalized and the hospital stripped
of all surgical instruments and equipment. It looked as
though this might have happened several weeks, even
months, earlier – there was just no way of knowing. Neither
was there any sign of human habitation anywhere near it.
But Mark was not downhearted. He hadn't really expected
to find anybody or anything at the mission.

It was time now for me to keep my side of the bargain. I
sent for Mark.

'We're going to stay in Aba for a minimum of fourteen
days, Mark,' I said. 'My next objective is Faradje, which is
due west sixty-five kilometres. I'll move when I'm ready. But
this is your moment. When you and your men have had a
good rest, I want you to make a thorough reconnaissance of
the area behind Aba, and then the country north along the
Sudan border for about one hundred kilometres. There's a
good track leading in that direction but it runs out after thirty

kilometres at a place called Missa. From there on you may
have to march. The whole thing may take you seven or eight
days. Even longer.'

His eyes lit up. At last, this was what he had come all this
way for.

'It is possible the enemy may have developed a new line
of communication from Faradje to the Sudan border, bypass-
ing Aba altogether. I want to know if this is so. If it is, watch
out. You could bump into heavy concentrations of enemy
troops. Remember, your task is reconnaissance only. Fight
if you have to protect yourselves, but don't get involved in a
fight with superior numbers. I won't be able to help you if
you do. Move fast. Go up along the border as far as you can
and then back here again by a different route. Do not approach Faradje from the north. We just don't know what we
are likely to find there. Got that?'

'Got it. But apart from that, I can go anywhere I like?'

'Yes. But that will depend on the amount of fuel you can
carry and what tracks there are. Think it out carefully and let
me have your general plan as soon as you can. Also a
nominal roll of everybody taking part. I shall want your
estimated day of return and the exact route you intend to use
on your approach to Aba. Let me know when you are ready
to go. Draw what maps you may need from Lieutenant
Germani. By the way, Mark, I think you can now confide in
Hans. You will find him the soul of discretion: he used to be
a medical doctor in Germany. During your absence he will
be interrogating the prisoners and can make enquiries about
Marylou. One of them may have seen her or heard something about her, you never know.'

I asked the Cubans to make an air recce at dawn the next
day and to let me know what enemy dispositions they could
see along the border, if any; what villages appeared to be well
inhabited, and any other relevant information which might
be of use to Mark.

By noon next day I gave it all to him. There was nothing
exceptional in it. Hans had also interrogated the Portuguese
who had been running the clinic in Aba for the rebels during
the last few months. He said that as far as he knew there were
one or two fairly large leper colonies along the Sudan border,
one almost up as far as the northern end of the Garamba
National Park. Some of the lepers used to come to Aba for

medicines from time to time but he hadn't seen any of them for a very long time. He thought they might have crossed into the Sudan. Apart from them he didn't think there were any big villages in the area.

Mark's plan was to leave at dawn the next morning. He came into my office for last-minute instructions just as the first rays of a blood-red sun were rising.

'Confident, Mark?'

'Yes, sir. If Marylou is anywhere in this area, I'm going to find her.'

'I'm sure you will Mark.' I shook his hand and put my hand on his shoulder. 'God speed you, my boy.'

A few moments later his unit had disappeared in a cloud of red dust. I watched them until they were out of sight behind the African Inland Mission, the buildings that Marylou must have known so well.

Hans began his interrogation of the prisoners. One or two of them knew about the lady doctor from Mungbere, some had heard of her, one had a strange story that she had become the wife of a Liotina, a rebel leader. I dismissed that immediately as rubbish. Hans was more cautious. In the field of military intelligence every item of information, no matter how ridiculous it might seem, had to be sifted and weighed. He did that now. He got the name of the Liotina. It was Boyulu. Nobody could tell him where Boyulu was. One man said he had been badly wounded when the 'Americans' bombed Paulis some weeks ago, and he thought he was killed in the raid. Another told him that Boyulu was one of several badly wounded men being evacuated to the Sudan from Faradje hospital. The truck had been machine-gunned from the air and burnt out. Everybody knew there were no survivors.

Mark returned nine days later. We debriefed him. He had patrolled the length of the Sudan border right up to the point where it joined the Garamba National Park. He had come back by another route. He had firm evidence that a new supply route existed from the Sudan to Faradje. He had spoken to dozens of villagers along the border. He had brought back seven of them for further interrogation. He had not fired a single shot. He had shown Marylou's photograph to many of the villagers but nobody had seen her. He had not found any leper colonies. I could tell from the slope of his shoulders that he was beginning to give up hope.

Even though Mark's report was mostly negative information, this also was of great value to us. As far as the search for Marylou was concerned, I told him, he must not forget that Faradje was a major town with its own hospital. The rebels would have wanted a doctor for that. Logically, she could be there. If not, then there was Dungu and after that Niangara, big towns away to the west. All these places lay on our route, all would have to be taken in due course before we could implement General Mobutu's plan of pacification and rehabilitation. Marylou could be in any one of those. He must hang in there. Be patient. The country was enormous.

A few days later we assaulted Faradje. It fell without a big battle, as the enemy had already spirited themselves away to the Sudan by their new escape and supply route. But Marylou was not at the hospital. Nobody had seen her or even heard of her. Mark became increasingly despondent, but he was made of good stuff and buoyed up continually by an inner conviction that told him he was going to find her in the end, or if not that, he would get some positive proof of her fate. He refused to give in. I was proud of him.

5 Commando settled into Faradje. I had my headquarters a little way out of town at the Roman Catholic mission, now deserted of course. The unit spent most of its time helping the civil authorities get the town going again. The native population was returning every day by the hundred.

One of the first persons of note to return was the bishop of Faradje, His Grace Sebastian Nkulu. The bishop was a small Pickwickian figure, right down to his gold-rimmed pince-nez. He was stout, happy and kind. He radiated goodness and love for his fellow men. I classed him as a practising Christian rather than a political one. As time went by, he invited me to the palace, which was well furbished but not as splendidly as its name might suggest. On some of those occasions we would end by discussing the state of the Congo and our fellow men.

One evening he asked me what I would suggest as a cure-all solution to the problems the Congo was experiencing. I certainly knew what they were. I had witnessed most of them at first hand. The main problem, it seemed to me, was that the peasant population was too ready to accept Communist doctrine at its face value; they were too easily persuaded that the state would take over all their problems; that they thought Christianity had nothing to offer them but restrictions on their easygoing way of life, the number of their wives, their night-time dancing; that they were prepared to regard the state as a father figure and all the God they would need in this life. Was it any wonder they were willing to embrace Communist doctrine with all it promised?

My solution to this problem was elementary but sincere. It amounted to one thing, education. After a primary education, I suggested, should come the learning of the Word. A thorough knowledge of the scriptures was basic to my belief that through a knowledge of the Bible, through Christianity, the Congolese people would become instruments of righteous change for their nation. Politics would play no part in this process. It was, as I saw it, the only real hope for the Congo, for Africa, perhaps even for the world. My view was, I suppose, naïve and over simplified, but the bishop helped me along whenever I got stuck with my thesis.

He had similar ideas but could express them with more precision and eloquence. Education, he agreed, was a desirable and necessary beginning, but it would take time, money and organization. Rare commodities, he said, with a sigh. That was, he agreed, the essential base from which to begin. In the meantime we must continue to teach and live the fundamental Christian doctrine – love one another: 'A new commandment I give unto you, That ye love one another; as I have loved you.'

An evening with the bishop was a cleansing experience, and fun. Our friendship was cemented the day I was browsing through his library and came across one of my favourite books, *Blandings Castle*, in French.

'Fancy that! You read P.G. Wodehouse, Your Grace?'

'*Bien sûr!*' he replied. '*Je suis un peu civilisé!*'

I laughed. If he thought of himself as a little civilized then the rest of us must be troglodytes!

Two nights later the orderly officer woke me just after midnight.

'Sorry to disturb you, sir. The bishop wants to see you as soon as he can. He is down at the cathedral.'

'Anything wrong?'

'He didn't say, but it sounds pretty urgent.'

I woke Hans and Mark Forrester. We jeeped down to the

palace and walked the hundred metres or so towards the cathedral. It was a stormy night. Heavy monsoon clouds careered across the sky at great speed, chased by a half gale. From time to time a full moon would break through to shine brilliantly, painting everything with a silvery glow. It was bright enough to cast a solid shadow. Near the great west door I could make out a small group of men, clustered together. Round them was another ring of people. One of them was the bishop. I could see his purple sash. I stopped close behind him. He said nothing but pointed to the inner group. I looked. The moon came out strongly at that moment and filled the yard with an unnaturally bright light. I felt a hand grip my left elbow. It was Hans. Another gripped my right. It was Mark.

In the middle of the circle of black men a white girl was standing, her hair matted, her clothes torn and dishevelled. On her face was a look of unutterable sadness as one by one each member of the group came up to her, knelt at her feet and kissed the hem of her tattered skirt. She placed her hands gently on their heads and spoke to them in turn, words of loving kindness. Now they knelt in a semicircle, in prayer, as she bade them goodbye. She spoke so softly I could hardly make out what she was saying. The bishop translated. "The Lord bless thee and keep thee: The Lord make his face to shine upon thee, and be gracious unto thee: the Lord lift up his countenance upon thee and give thee peace." Farewell, my dear, dear friends. I shall never forget you. Never. And thank you.'

They withdrew one at a time into the darkness of the passage by the west door. My heart was thumping.

'My God!' I said, shocked. 'Can it be?'

Mark Forrester, that man of iron, the quiet hero of a dozen actions, had broken down in tears, one hand covering his face.

'It is. It's Marylou!' he sobbed, choking back his tears. 'Dear God! What have they done to her?'

Nobody moved. I found it impossible to look away from that beautiful alabastrine face, filled as it was with compassion and suffering, while the bishop told us the story. The villagers had brought the young girl in barely an hour ago. She was the only survivor of a truck that had been blasted from the air. They had found her wandering in the bush last

November, three months ago. They had taken her to their village, looked after her and protected her from the rebels. Now they heard the rebels had gone, they had brought her back.

It was a heroic story. My first impulse was to meet the men, to reward them, to help them in some way, to repay them for their deeds of kindness. I walked quickly over to their leader, a tiny, shrivelled man, standing in front of the others in the darkness of the stone passage leading to the great western door. They all held their cloaks in front of their faces. As I approached, they began to back away, nervously. I came up to the head man and drew the cloak gently from his face, to get a proper look at him. Simultaneously, as though on a signal, all the others dropped their cloaks. I drew back, involuntarily. They were all lepers. The blotched whiteness of their skins, their noses and ears and fingers eaten away by the deadly disease told their hideous story. But I had seen it all before, many times, and it didn't stop me from thanking them from the bottom of my heart.

I went back to Hans and Mark. Hans was concerned. We must treat the girl very gently, he said. It would be a great error to bombard her with questions and explanations until she felt safe again and had accepted she was back among friends. I asked him to go forward and speak to her. I stayed with Mark. Hans approached the solitary figure quietly and removed his beret.

'Dr Daintree?'

'Yes.'

'Welcome home! I am Dr Hans Germani. You are among friends. We want only to help you. This is the bishop of Faradje. That is my commanding officer over there. You are safe with us. There are no rebel forces here. We are going to look after you now. But do you think ... you are strong enough to stand another very happy shock?'

She raised a small, forlorn smile.

'I'll try. I hope so.'

Out of the shadows came Mark. He took her in his arms. We left them alone as they wept with joy and relief, neither saying a word, Marylou secure and happy in the warmth of Mark's strong embrace. It was a sacred moment. Prayer had been answered. And we knew it.

It was obvious to Hans that the girl was in desperate need

of medical attention. She had just walked over 150 kilometres through the bush; her feet were torn and bleeding. Mark picked her up and carried her back to the bishop's palace like a baby, her arms round his neck. She was weak and terribly emaciated but radiantly happy. From time to time he would stop to give her a rest, and she would whisper, 'The Lord has answered my prayers! Jesus has answered my prayers!'

The bishop, beaming happily on all around him, exclaimed joyfully, 'It's a miracle, a veritable miracle!' Then he arranged for Marylou to be given a room and to be nursed by his staff. After a little happy talk and on a discreet signal from Hans we took our leave. Mark was left to watch over her right through the night.

Back at my headquarters I sent a signal to the military attaché, US embassy, Léopoldville:

> *Immediate stop For Colonel Raudstein stop US citizen Marylou Daintree recovered from bush 0130 hours today stop grateful send four-seater aircraft Faradje soonest stop regards Mike OC 5 Commando Faradje.*

The following day, just after noon, a Beachcraft Baron buzzed my headquarters. We dashed out to the airstrip. The two-engined four-seater plane waddled across the uneven grass and stopped in front of us. Major Dick Kohlbrand stepped out and saluted. We shook hands.

'Got here as soon as I could, Mike,' he said. 'Knut says to say thank you. How's our brave little lady?'

Marylou was too weak to make the 2,000 kilometre journey back to Léopoldville that day so, on Hans' advice, we delayed her departure by forty-eight hours. But knowing a little about American girls I sent for my RSM.

'Sergeant Major, have we by any chance a ladies' hairdresser in 5 Commando?'

'Dunno, sir, but I'll look into it at once. That queer lad Ellis could be one, I shouldn't wonder.'

Volunteer Ellis, one of our medical orderlies, was shown in.

'Alice,' I said (it was his *nom de guerre*, believe it or not,) 'this is something special. I want you to do a young lady's hair. And I want you to do the very best job you can, just to please me. Do you think you can do that?'

'Of course, sir. For you, anything! But listen, dear – I mean, Colonel, what about the shampoo and the hair-drier and all those things I shall need? Goodness, I've got the reputation of Salon Delphine, Salisbury, to keep up, haven't I?'

The next day Hans and I walked down to see how Marylou was making out. Hans wanted her to talk about her experiences if she felt able, and not to bottle them up. He felt it would do her good to tell us about them, perhaps for the last time. Her story amazed us.

On the day of her arrival in Faradje last November she had been ordered to operate on a senior official of the rebel movement who had been seriously wounded. As soon as he was able to make the journey he was to be taken in a four-wheel-drive vehicle to a secret rendezvous on the Sudan border, a place about one hundred kilometres north of Faradje. She had sat in the back with the patient strapped into a stretcher alongside her, an officer of the APL and the driver in front. The vehicle was loaded down with cans of fuel for the return journey. There were no tracks but the terrain was not difficult. It was just a matter of avoiding obstructions and maintaining a certain direction. The officer navigated by compass. They ground along in low gear, stopping whenever the water in the radiator boiled. They were making no more than ten to fifteen kilometres in the hour.

At midday, when they were about twenty kilometres from the border, a number of fighter aircraft flew high over them. The driver made a dash for cover but it was too late, they had been spotted. Three of the planes dive-bombed them and straddled the truck with bullets, one of them making a direct hit. The fuel cans exploded. Marylou found herself lying on the sand ten metres away, watching helplessly as the truck blazed fiercely. All three of its occupants were burned to death. She crawled away into the bush. After an hour or so she recovered and began to walk in a northerly direction, hoping she would come eventually to the people they had been on their way to meet. But she saw nobody. Not a person, not an animal, not a bird, not an insect. The whole world was empty, pitilessly hot and still.

It was loose reddish sand and savannah as far as she could see, the horizon broken only by the profile of a flat-topped acacia or borassus palm. The direct heat of the sun was unbearable. A shimmering haze restricted her visibility to less than 500 metres. Her vision began to fail. She felt as though she had a massive migraine. She rested under a bush, made a determined effort to calm herself, willed herself not to panic and to put her trust in the Lord. She prayed intensely for help. As soon as the sun went down she began to walk again, realizing she must find help before her strength gave out. She halted just after dawn, exhausted, and looked for something to protect her from the sun.

Twenty-four hours later, without food or water, she collapsed. All she could tell us of that nightmare journey was how she had tried to hide from the blistering sun, how she covered herself with sand or tried to tunnel her way under a bush. But the desert beat her in the end. Delirious, she began to wander. How many days later she does not know, but eventually a group of villagers foraging for firewood far from their village, found her wandering, half demented and on the point of death from dehydration. She knows now that the good Lord watched over her or she would surely have perished.

They carried her to their village of reed huts enclosed within a high stockade, where they nursed her slowly back to health. The sun was their life-long enemy. They knew from bitter experience how to treat sunstroke, heatstroke and exhaustion. Carefully they brought her back to life and sanity. What little they had they shared with her, generously, with compassion. After two weeks she was able to talk again. A week later she began to walk. She was not frightened and placed her faith in the Lord. She knew He had sent her here for some purpose.

This, she told us, soon became apparent. The small group of people who had saved her life were lepers, all in an advanced state of the disease. They had some medicines but not enough or the skill to apply them. She began to minister to them, physically and spiritually. Her eyes sparkled when she told us of the wonderful day when they truly believed they were God's children, that in the next life He would give them beautiful clean bodies and they would be the same as everybody else, not shunned. No longer would they be called 'the ones apart'.

They had rescued her, she said, and she had rescued them. In the process she had been able to fulfil her ministry, a gift from the Lord not given to very many of His willing workers.

For her part she had been privileged to teach the villagers something more precious than anything they could ever have hoped for, a knowledge of Jesus Christ.

Some months later they heard that the rebels had left Faradje. The leader of the little group called a meeting. They decided they must make the long journey back to Faradje with their teacher, much as they would have liked her to stay with them for ever. Every man, woman and child took to the bush and escorted her safely back to civilization.

This was the moment for the bishop to show his temporal power. With the efficiency for which he was justly famous, he gave orders to build a leprosarium immediately, as an extension to the hospital. He insisted that these men, women and children, 'the ones apart', as they called themselves, should live there from that day on. He didn't know where the money would come from to finance this additional burden on his slender resources, he said, but he knew the Lord would provide. Mark took him on one side, and after a quiet chat the bishop came back, unable to keep the good news to himself a moment longer, to announce with a burst of laughter that the new leprosarium was to be financed by a distant well-wisher who preferred to remain anonymous, out of gratitude for all the villagers had done for Marylou. Another miracle had happened! Hans and I knew the miracle would without a doubt have its roots in Austin, Texas.

Every day thereafter the bishop sent one of his curates to visit the lepers and to continue their instruction in the Word. After a time they lost their despair and desolation, and no longer called themselves 'the ones apart'. They told the bishop they had been led by the Lord to find the light at Faradje. It was a miracle indeed.

A group of forty or fifty men gathered at the airstrip as a send-off party for Marylou two days later. They cheered and clapped in unfeigned admiration when they saw her emerge slowly from the back of a truck, swathed in cottonwool, bandages and blankets. Mark carried her gently to the plane. More than enough willing hands helped to snug her down in the Beachcraft. She looked rested but more delicate than ever. Alice was still fussing round her, exercising the proprietary rights his status as her hairdresser had conferred on him.

Marylou's entire worldly possessions amounted to one

Bible which the bishop had given her. She had asked us all to sign the flyleaf. I was sending Mark with her, officially, as her escort. Only Hans and I knew I had let him break his contract. He saluted.

'Thank you, Colonel. Thank you for everything. Thank you too, Hans.'

'We must thank you, Mark,' said Hans. 'You have been a lesson to us all in courage and fortitude.'

He looked slightly embarrassed.

'Colonel, may I just say one thing before I go?'

'Please do, Mark. Go ahead.'

'You were wrong, you know. You remember when you told me at Bunia I wouldn't learn anything from 5 Commando. Well, I have. I don't just mean military stuff, but something much more important. I've made good friends, and I've taken a real pride in leading my men. They're like ... they're like family. It has been an honour serving with you and' – he found it a little hard to say; he was after all an officer in the US Marine Corps, – 'I love you all. Goodbye and may the good Lord protect you.'

I shook his hand for the last time and handed him a sealed cardboard box which I asked him to give to Marylou, but only when she had quite recovered, mentally and physically. It was her diary.

The major taxied down the field as we waved farewell. We stood there mesmerized long after the plane had vanished into the blue and white horizon, reluctant to move.

We walked back to my headquarters, slowly, in the sunshine. Hans, my intellectual friend, was unusually pensive. Like me he had been struck with the ethereal beauty of Marylou Daintree. It had left us bemused. Neither of us had ever encountered anything like it in our lives before. It was a beauty inspired by some indefinable glow of goodness. And now that she had gone we felt unaccountably deprived of something precious and desirable.

'Keats, Colonel,' said Hans, eventually, as though he had solved all our problems. '"Beauty is truth, truth beauty, – that is all ye know on earth, and all ye need to know."'

Index